COLLINS
PHRASE BOOKS

GERMAN

Collins Phrase Books

FRENCH
GERMAN
ITALIAN
PORTUGUESE
SPANISH
SCANDINAVIAN
RUSSIAN
GREEK
YUGOSLAV
DUTCH
LATIN AMERICAN SPANISH

COLLINS
PHRASE BOOKS

GERMAN

Compiled by
GERDA WILLIAMSON

COLLINS
LONDON AND GLASGOW

First Published 1964
This Edition 1965
Latest Reprint 1978

Cover photographs for cased
edition by courtesy of
Picturepoint Ltd. (top right)
J. Allan Cash Ltd. (top left and bottom)

ISBN Cased 0 00 433903 7
ISBN Limp 0 00 433923 1

CONTENTS

5

INHALT

CONTENTS

INTRODUCTION

The selection of words and phrases compiled in this edition, should enable the traveller visiting Germany, Austria and the German-speaking parts of Switzerland, to avoid misunderstandings when shopping, ordering a meal or perhaps trying to find his way.

The clear and accurate pronunciation of every word may be read simply as English syllables, and the use of confusing symbols is avoided.

Currency

There are no restrictions on the amount of foreign currency imported into or exported from Germany and Switzerland. Austria, however, restricts the export of local currency to 15,000 Austrian Schillings.

Travellers Cheques may be readily cashed at large hotels, good restaurants and high class shops. It is advisable to carry a certain amount of local currency for incidental expenses on the journey.

Tipping

In Germany and Austria a service charge of 10-15 per cent is always added to bills in hotels and restaurants but it is customary to give tips over and above the obligatory service charge.

In Switzerland tips are included in all inclusive rates; in all other cases they will be added to the bill separately. Additional tips are given only for special services.

Forms of Address

When addressing strange people to ask the way, etc., one should begin "Verzeihen Sie" (fair-tsī'-en zee); a lady is addressed politely as "Gnädige Frau" (g-nay'-dig-*er* frow), where Madam would be used in English. If she is unmarried the correct address is "Gnädiges Fräulein" (g-nay'-dig-ez froy'-line).

Shop assistants, telephone operators, waitresses, etc., are addressed as "Fräulein". "Herr" and "Frau" are used only in connection with the name, like "Mr." or "Mrs."

Entertainment

There is a rich assortment of entertainment available in Germany. The standard of productions is high, and music in particular is usually excellent. The lighter side of music, in the form of the "Operette", generally offers good entertainment, and does not demand a knowledge of German to the same extent as does a straight play.

The music hall "Variété" is very good, on the whole, and much of it may be enjoyed by one who does not know much German.

In Austria festivals (Festspiele) are held in many towns and villages during the summer season.

German-speaking Switzerland

The German spoken in Switzerland sounds very different from that of Germany, but in talking to foreign visitors the Swiss will adapt his pronunciation accordingly.

In dealing with Swiss German it may be helpful to remember the following points. The chief differences in pronunciation between Swiss German and standard German are in the vowel sounds.

German au (ow) is pronounced (oo) in Swiss German;
    thus German aus (owce) sounds like (oos).

German ei (i) is pronounced (ee), so that eis (ice) sounds like (ees).

NOTE ON PRONUNCIATION SCHEME

The pronunciation of German, like that of our own language, varies widely in different parts of the country. This book is based on the standard pronunciation as used on the stage, and it will be generally understood.

The pronunciations given should be read simply as English words and phrases, with the stress placed on the syllable immediately preceding the accent mark ('). Since in some cases the pronunciation of a group of letters may differ in English according to the word in which it occurs, and since one or two German sounds cannot be accurately represented in English, the following simple rules should be remembered:

a—The German short "a" is represented by u, pronounced as in trunk (the open sound used in the South of England). It is pronounced roughly like the "a" in North of England dialects.

i, o—In general the correct value is given to the vowels "i" and "o" if the pronunciation is read as in English words. In cases of doubt a stroke is placed over the letter:

    ī, ō, denote the long sound as in write, note.

A mute "e" is often added to a syllable to give the correct pronunciation, and should be pronounced as in English.

For example: Streit = shtrite (as in English kite)
             der   = dare (as in English).

ow is always to be pronounced as in cow and not as in show

ü—This sound is the English "ee" made with the lips forward and rounded (in whistling position).

o͞o—represents a shortened form of the English oo as in foot. Thus the German pronunciation of the "u" in unter (o͞on'-ter) is similar to that of the North of England under. The unmarked oo is pronounced as in English boot.

er, ur—The italic r should not be pronounced; it is added to give the correct quality of the vowel preceding it.

Thus German e at the end of a word, represented by "er", is to be pronounced as a separate syllable with a sound as in English latter.

"ur" is the German ö sound. For example, schön (shurn), rather like the English urn.

r—It is important to note that the German r should be trilled (as in Scots). Thus, "warm" (varm) should be pronounced "varrrm".

ch is pronounced as the English "sh", but with the lips drawn back.

CH represents the gutteral sound as in Scots loch, and is always used after the vowels a, o, u.

g is always hard, as in English get.

y is to be sounded as in English yes.

o͞n is used in words pronounced with the French nasal.

GRAMMATICAL NOTES

German nouns are either masculine, feminine or neuter. All nouns begin with a capital letter. Inanimate objects have no general rule, therefore it is advisable to remember each noun with its article.

the table   — der Tisch (masculine)
the door   — die Tür (feminine)
the window — das Fenster (neuter)

Definite Article

In German the definite article is determined by the gender of the noun,

der — before a masculine singular noun
die — before a feminine singular or a plural noun
das — before a neuter singular noun

Examples:

der Mann—the man, die Frau—the woman, das Kind—the child, die Männer—the men.

finite Article

ndefinite article in German (*a* and *an* in English) also changes with the gender of the noun.

ein — before a masculine or neuter noun
eine — before a feminine noun
    ein Mann—a man, eine Frau—a woman, ein Kind—a child

Plural Forms

The plural of a noun is usually formed by adding:
e to the singular of masculine nouns,
    der Hund—the dog, die Hunde—the dogs
n to the singular of masculine nouns ending with e,
    der Junge—the boy, die Jungen—the boys
n or *en* to the singular of feminine nouns,
    die Strasse—the street, die Strassen—the streets
    die Frau—the woman, die Frauen—the women
er or *e* to the singular of neuter nouns,
    das Kind—the child, die Kinder—the children
    das Netz—the net, die Netze—the nets

Exceptions are:

(1) Nouns which have *a, o, u* or *au* in the stem, change *a* to *ä*, *o* to *ö*, *u* to *ü*, *au* to *äu* and add *e* or *er*.
    Mann—man, Männer—men
    Sohn—son, Söhne—sons
    Stuhl—chair, Stühle—chairs
    Haus—house, Häuser—houses

(2) Masculine and neuter nouns ending with *el, en* or *er* generally do not change,
    der Löffel—the spoon, die Löffel—the spoons
    der Kragen—the collar, die Kragen—the collars
    das Messer—the knife, die Messer—the knives

Possessive Adjectives

The masculine, feminine, neuter and plural nouns determine the change of the adjective as shown below:

	Masculine and Neuter	*Feminine and Plural*
my	mein	meine
your	dein	deine
his	sein	seine
her	ihr	ihre
our	unser	unsere
your	Ihr	Ihre
their	ihr	ihre

Demonstrative Adjectives

In German the demonstrative adjectives change their endings to agree with masculine, feminine, neuter or plural nouns.

	Masculine	*Neuter*	*Feminine and Plural*	
this } that }	dieser	dieses	diese	{ these { those
that	jener	jenes	jene	those

> Ich kenne diesen Mann—I know this (that) man
> Ich kenne jene Frau—I know that woman

Verbs

The subject of verbs is too extensive and complicated to be discussed in detail in a phrase book. Therefore only some essential forms of verbs in common use are given.

It is important to remember that in German the second person singular *du* (you) is only used when addressing relations, close friends and children. The second person plural *Sie* (you) is always used when addressing strangers. Note that this form of verb is always spelled with a capital letter.

For a past action either the Imperfect or the Perfect can be used. The Perfect is formed by the present tense of *sein* (to be) or *haben* (to have) followed by the Past Participle. In conversation the Perfect is more frequently used.

	Imperfect	*Perfect*
I saw	ich sah	ich habe gesehen
I was	ich war	ich bin gewesen

The future tense is formed by using *werden* (shall) plus the Infinitive of the verb.

> I shall see—ich werde sehen

SEIN (ZINE)—TO BE

Present Tense	*Past Tense*	*Future Tense*
Ich bin	ich war	ich werde sein
du bist	du warst	du wirst sein
er ist	er war	er wird sein
sie ist	sie war	sie wird sein
wir sind	wir waren	wir werden sein
Sie sind	Sie waren	Sie werden sein
sie sind	sie waren	sie werden sein

HABEN (HAH'-BEN)—TO HAVE

Present Tense	*Past Tense*	*Future Tense*
ich habe	ich hatte	ich werde haben
du hast	du hattest	du wirst haben
er hat	er hatte	er wird haben
sie hat	sie hatte	sie wird haben
wir haben	wir hatten	wir werden haben
Sie haben	Sie hatten	Sie werden haben
sie haben	sie hatten	sie werden haben

SAGEN (ZAHG'-EN)—TO SAY

Present Tense	*Past Tense*	*Future Tense*
ich sage	ich sagte	ich werde sagen
du sagst	du sagtest	du wirst sagen
er sagt	er sagte	er wird sagen
sie sagt	sie sagte	sie wird sagen
wir sagen	wir sagten	wir werden sagen
Sie sagen	Sie sagten	Sie werden sagen
sie sagen	sie sagten	sie werden sagen

Personal Pronouns

The Subject or Nominative of the personal pronouns (*ich, du, er, sie, wir, Sie, sie*) have been used in the verb tables. When used as direct object (Accusative) the pronouns are,

mich — me		uns — us	
dich — you		Sie — you	
ihn — him		sie — them	
sie — her			

I call him—ich rufe ihn

When used as indirect object (Dative) the pronouns are,

mir — me, to me	uns — us, to us
dir — you, to you	Ihnen — you, to you
ihm — him, to him	ihnen — them, to them
ihr — her, to her	

ich gebe ihm den Brief—I give (to) him the letter

Relative Pronouns

The form of the relative pronouns is determined by the gender of the noun they are referring to.

who } der, welcher (referring to masculine noun)
which } die, welche (referring to feminine or plural noun)
that } das, welches (referring to neuter noun)
  der Mann, der (welcher) . . . — the man who . . .
  die Frau, die (welche) . . . — the woman who . . .
  das Haus, das (welches) . . . — the house which (that) . . .
  die Kinder, die (welche) . . . — the children who . . .

Interrogative Pronouns

  wer?—who? (Nominative)
  wessen?—whose? (Genitive)
  wen?—whom? (Accusative)
  wem?—to whom? (Dative)
 Wer ist da?—Who is there?
 Wessen Buch?—Whose book?
 Wen haben Sie gesehen?—Whom did you see?
 Wem haben Sie es gegeben?—To whom did you give it?

What, followed by a noun, is in German:
  was für ein (before a masculine noun)
  was für eine (before a feminine noun)
  was für ein (before a neuter noun)

   What man?—Was für ein Mann?
   What kind of a door?—Was für eine Tür?

Indefinite Pronoun

One, *they* and *people*, used indefinitely, are translated in German by
'man.'

   One can buy it—man kann es kaufen.
   People say—man sagt.

COMMON WORDS AND PHRASES

VOCABULARY

above, über (ü-ber)
after, nach (naCH)
against, gegen (gay-gen)
all, alle (ull'-er)
almost, fast, beinahe (fust, by-nah'-er)
among, unter (ŏŏnt'-er)
before, in front of, vor (for)
behind, hinter (hin'-ter)
below, unter (ŏŏn'-ter)
beside, neben (nay'-ben)
between, zwischen (tsvi'-shen)
downstairs, unten (ŏŏn'-ten)
elsewhere, anderswo (un'-ders-vo)
enough, genug (ger-noog)
everybody, jeder (yay'-der)
everything, alles (ull'-ez)
everywhere, überall (ü'-ber-ull)
except, ausser (owce'-er)
far, weit (vite)
for, für (für)
here, hier (here)
how, wie (vee)
how many ⎫
how much ⎭ wieviel (vee-feel)
in, into, in (in)
inside, drinnen (drin'-en)
left, links (links)
less, weniger (vane'-ig-er)
little, klein, wenig (kline, vay'-nich)
much, many, viel, viele (feel, feel'-er)
more, mehr (mair)
near, nahe (nah'-er)
on, auf (owf)
outside, draussen (drowce'-en)
over there, dort drüben (dort drüb'-en)
right, rechts (rechts)
somebody, jemand (yay'-munt)
something, etwas (et'-vuss)
there, da, dort (dah, dawrt)
through, durch (dŏŏrch)
too many, too much, zuviel (tsŏŏ'-feel)
towards, gegen (gay-gen)
until, bis (biss)

17

upstairs, oben (ō'-ben)
very, sehr (zair)
when, wann, wenn (vunn, venn)
where, wo (voh)
why, warum (vah-rŏŏm)
with, mit (mit)
without, ohne (ō'-ner)

POLITE EXPRESSIONS

Yes. No
                     Ja. Nein
                     yah, nine

Please. Thank you
                   Bitte. Danke
             bitt'-er, dunk'-er

N.B. *When declining an offer, Germans do not say "No, thank you," but
simply "Danke", if one wishes to accept, say, a second helping at the
table, one should say "Bitte".*

Good morning
                  Guten Morgen
            goot'-en morg'en

Good afternoon
                  Guten Tag
            goot'-en tahg

Good evening. Good night
           Guten Abend. Gute Nacht
                     (*familiar*)
       goot'-en ah'-bent, goot'-er naCHt

Good-bye
                  Auf Wiedersehen
           owf vee'-der-zay-en

Excuse me please }
I am sorry }
                  Entschuldigen Sie bitte
                     Verzeihen Sie
      ent-shool-dig-en zee bitt-er, fair-tsi'-en zee

Don't mention it
                  Bitte
            bitt-er

I beg your pardon ? (*for some-*   Wie bitte?
   thing not heard)
                  vee bitt'-er

I am very sorry
                  Ich bedauere sehr
        ich bed-ow'-er-er zair

Can I help you ?	Kann ich Ihnen behilflich sein?
	kun ich ee'-nen be-hilf-lich zine
Please sit down	Bitte setzen Sie sich
	bitt'-er zet-sen Zee sich
Help yourself !	Bedienen Sie sich!
	be-deenen Zee sich
How are you ?	Wie geht es Ihnen?
	vee gate ez ee'-nen
Very well—and you ?	Sehr gut und Ihnen?
	zair goot ōōnt ee'-nen
Allow me to introduce you to . . .	Darf ich Ihnen . . . vorstellen
	darf ich ee'-nen . . . fore'-shtell-en
Delighted to meet you	Sehr angenehm
	zair un'-gen-alm
Congratulations	Glückwünsche
	glück-vünshe
Am I disturbing you ?	Störe ich?
	shtur'-rer ich
Allow me! You are very kind	Darf ich! Sie sind sehr gütig
	darf ich! zee zint zair güt'-ich
It's all the same to me	Es macht mir nichts aus
	ez maCHt mere nichts owce
Don't worry	Machen Sie sich keine Sorgen
	maCH'-en zee zich ki'-ner zor'-gen
Your good health	Prosit
	pro'-zeet
Thank you for your hospitality	Vielen Dank für Ihre Gastfreundschaft
	feel'-en dunk' für ee'-rer gust'-froynt-shuft
We had a very good time	Es hat uns sehr gefallen
	ez hut ōōns zair gef'-ull'-en
We are (I am) much obliged to you	Wir sind (ich bin) Ihnen sehr verbunden
	vere zint, ich bin, ee'-nen zair fair-bōōnd-'en

GENERAL DIFFICULTIES

Do you speak English ?   Sprechen Sie englisch?

shprech'-en zee eng'-lish

I do not speak German   Ich spreche nicht deutsch

ich shprech'-er nicht doytsh

Can anyone speak English ?   Spricht jemand englisch?

shpricht yay'-munt eng'-lish

I do not understand   Ich verstehe nicht

ich fair-shtay'-er nicht

Will you please speak more slowly?   Bitte sprechen Sie langsamer?

bitt'-er shprech'-en zee lung'-zahm-er

Write it down, please   Bitte schreiben Sie es auf

bitt'-er shri'-ben zee ez owf

What does that mean ?   Was bedeutet das?

vuss be-doi'tet duss

What is that in German ?   Wie heisst das auf deutsch?

vee hisst duss owf doytsh

What do you want?   Was wünschen Sie?

vuss vün'-shen zee

This book may help you to explain it   Dieses Buch erklärt es Ihnen vielleicht

dee'-zez booCH air-klairt ez ee'-nen feel-licht

Where are we going?   Wohin gehen wir?

vo-hin' gay'-en vere

I have lost . . .   Ich habe . . . verloren

ich hah'ber . . . fair-lo'-ren

I will give you my address   Ich gebe Ihnen meine Adresse

ich gay'-ber ee'-nen mi'-ner ad-dress'-er

What is your name ?   Wie heissen Sie?

vee hiss'-en zee

What is your address ?   Wo wohnen Sie?

voh vo'-nen zee

Help ! Fire ! Thief !	Hilfe! Feuer! Dieb !

hil'-fer! foy'er! deep!

Come quickly and see . . .	Kommen Sie schnell und sehen Sie . . .

komm'-en zee shnell öont zay'-en zee . . .

My bag has been stolen	Meine Tasche ist gestohlen worden

mī'-ner tush'-er ist ger'-shtole-en vord'-en

That man is following me everywhere	Dieser Mann kommt mir überall nach

dee-zer mun kommt mere ü'-ber-ull naCH

Shall I call a policeman?	Soll ich einen Polizisten rufen?

zoll ich i'-nen pol-its-ist-en roof-en

Bring a policeman	Holen Sie einen Schutzmann

hole-en zee i'-nen shoots'-mun

I shall stay here	Ich bleibe hier

ich blī'-ber here

Will you help me?	Helfen Sie mir bitte

hell'-fen zee mere bitt'-er

Beware of . . .	Vorsicht . . .

for-sicht . . .

I don't know you	Ich kenne Sie nicht

ich kenn'-er zee nicht

I don't want to speak to you	Ich will mit Ihnen nicht sprechen

ich vill mit ee'-nen nicht shprech'-en

Leave me alone	Lassen Sie mich in Ruhe

luss'-en zee mich in roo'-er

That will do	Das ist genug

duss ist ger'-noog

Is this the right way to . . . ?	Komme ich auf diesem Wege nach . . . ?

komm'-er ich owf dee'-zem vaig'-er naCH . . .

Please can you tell me ?	Bitte, können Sie mir sagen?

bitt'-er, kurn'-en zee mere zahg'-en

Keep straight on Immer gerade aus
imm'-er ger-rah'-der owce

First on the right Die Erste rechts
dee airst'-er rechts

Second on the left Die Zweite links
dee tsvī'-ter links

Where is the W.C. ? Wo ist die Toilette?
vo ist dee twa-lett'-er

You are mistaken Sie haben sich geirrt
zee hah'-ben sich ger'-irrt

I didn't do it Ich habe es nicht getan
ich hah'-ber ez nicht ger'-tahn

I will give you nothing Ich werde Ihnen nichts geben
ich vair'-der ee'-nen nichts gay'-ben

It is very annoying Es ist sehr ärgerlich
ez ist zair air-ger-lich

It has nothing to do with me Das geht mich nichts an
duss gate mich nichts un

Where should one apply? An wen kann man sich wenden?
un vane kunn mun sich venn'-den

What must I do Was soll ich machen
vuss zoll ich maCHen

I have done nothing Ich habe nichts gemacht
ich hah'-ber nichts ger'-maCHt

I have already paid you Ich habe bereits bezahlt
ich hah'-ber ber'-īts ber'-tsahlt

I have paid you enough Ich habe genug bezahlt
ich hah'-ber ger'-noog ber'-tsahlt

Let me pass Lassen Sie mich vorbei
luss'-en zee mich for-by

Where is the Police Station ? Wo ist die Polizeiwache?
vo ist dee pol-eet-si-vuCH'-er

Where is the British Consulate ? Wo ist das englische Konsulat?
vo ist duss eng'-lish-er kon-zool-aht

MISCELLANEOUS EXPRESSIONS

Look down there (up there)	Sehen Sie dort unten (dort oben)
	zay'-en zee dort ōōnt'-en (dort oh-ben)
Because. Because of	Weil. Wegen
	vile, vay'-gen
That's it	Das ist das
	duss ist duss
It's too much	Es ist zuviel
	ez ist tsoo-feel
It's very cheap	Es ist sehr billig
	ez ist zair bill'-ich
Quickly. Slowly	Schnell. Langsam
	shnell, lahng'-sahm
Forward. Back	Vorwärts. Zurück
	for-vairts, tsoo-rück
On this side. On the other side	Auf dieser Seite. Auf der anderen Seite
	owf dee'-zer zi'-ter, owf dair un'-dair-en zi'-ter
As soon as possible	So bald wie möglich
	zo bult vee murg'-lich
At the latest	Spätestens
	shpate'-est-ens
Come in!	Herein!
	hair-ine'
Don't forget	Vergessen Sie nicht
	fair-guess'-en zee nicht
Hardly ever	Kaum
	kowm
I believe so	Ich glaube
	ich glow'-ber
I don't know	Ich weiss nicht
	ich vice nicht

I don't want it	Nein danke
	nine dunk'er
I hope	Ich hoffe
	ich hoff'-er
I see !	Ach so!
	aCH zo
Is it not so ?	Nicht wahr?
	nicht var
Listen to me	Hören Sie
	hur'-ren zee
Look out !	Passen Sie auf !
	pus'-sen zee owf
More or less	Mehr oder weniger
	mair ō'-der vay'-nig-er
Not so fast	Nicht so schnell
	nicht zo shnell
On the contrary	Im Gegenteil
	im gay-gen-tile
Wait a minute please	Bitte, warten Sie einen Moment
	bitt'-er, var'ten zee i'-nen mo-ment
I am in a hurry	Ich habe es eilig
	ich hah'ber ez i'-lich
What is that for ?	Wofür ist das?
	vo-für' ist duss
What is the matter ?	Was ist los?
	vuss ist loce
This doesn't work	Es geht nicht
	ez gait nicht
It is fine (bad) weather	Es ist schönes (schlechtes) Wetter
	ez ist shurn'-es (shlech'-tes) vett'-er
Very well. That's all	Sehr gut. Das ist Alles
	zair goot. duss ist ull'-es
Whose turn is it?	Wer ist dran?
	vair ist drun

To think of something	An etwas denken
	un et'-vuss denk'-en
By chance	Zufällig
	tsoo-fell-ich
It's not my fault	Es ist nicht meine Schuld
	ez ist nicht mī'-ner shoolt
One does one's best	Man tut sein Bestes
	mun toot zīne best'-es
Like this. Like that	So
	zo
You are right. You are wrong	Sie haben Recht. Sie haben Unrecht
	zee hah'-ben recht. zee hah'-ben ŏŏn'-recht

POPULAR IDIOMS

It's terribly funny	Es ist ulkig
	ez ist oolk'-ich
You're pulling my leg	Sie führen mich an
	zee für'-en mich un
You don't say!	Na, so etwas
	nah, zo et'-vuss
Agreed. O.K.	In Ordnung
	in ord'-nŏŏng
Likeable, nice (personality)	Nett
	nett
It's wonderful, splendid	Es ist herrlich
	ez ist hair'-lich
My pals	Meine Freunde
	mī'-ner froynd'-er
It's rotten luck	Das ist Pech
	duss ist pech
To put one's foot in it	Sich blamieren
	zich blah-mere'-en

To do something stupid	Etwas Dummes tun
	et'-vuss dōōm'-es toon
Things are going badly	Es sind schlechte Zeiten
	ez zint shlecht'-er tsite'-en
I am bored	Ich langweile mich
	ich lung-vile-er mich
What a pity	Wie schade
	vee shahd'-er
You will get used to it	Sie werden sich daran gewöhnen
	zee vaird'-en sich dah-run ger-vurn'-en
He was drunk. Idiot	Er war betrunken. Idiot
	air vahr ber'-trōōnk-en. ee-dee-oat
Take it easy!	Langsam!
	lung-zahm
Be quiet! Shut up!	Seien Sie ruhig! Halten Sie den Mund!
	zī-en zee rooh-ig! hult'-en zee dane mōōnt!
That's going too far	Das geht zu weit
	duss gait tsoo vīte
Damn!	Verdammt!
	fair-dumt'

PUBLIC NOTICES AND COMMON PHRASES

Abteil für Schwerbeschädigte	Compartment reserved for use of disabled
	up'-tile für shvair'-besh-aid'-ich-ter
Achtung !	Attention!
	aCH'tōōng
Alles aussteigen (einsteigen, umsteigen)	All out (all aboard, all change)
	ull'-ez owce'-shtīgen (ine'-shtī-gen, ōōm'-shtī-gen)
Auskunft (Büro)	Information (Office)
	owce'-kōōnft bü-ro

Äusserlich zu gebrauchen	For external use only (on medicine bottles)
oyss'-er-lich tsoo geb-rowCH'-en	
Autobahn	Motorway
ow'-to-bahn	
Bahnhofsvorsteher	Station-master
bahn'-höfs-fore-shtay-er	
Besetzt	Engaged (on doors)
ber-zetst'	
Damen (toilette)	Ladies (toilet)
dah'-men (twa-lett'-er)	
Das Betreten des Rasens ist verboten	Keep off the grass
duss ber-tray'-ten dez rah'-zenz ist fair-boat'-en	
Das Sprechen mit dem Fahrer während der Fahrt ist verboten	It is forbidden to speak to the driver during the journey
duss shprech'-en mit dame far'-er vay'-rent dair fahrt ist fair-boat'-en	
Drücken	Press, push (on bells, doors, etc.)
drük'-en	
Durchgangszug	Corridor train
döorch'-gungz-tsoog	
Einbahnstrasse	One-way street
ine'-bahn-shtrahss-er	
Eintritt frei	Admission free
ine'-tritt fry	
Fahrkarten (in Switzerland, Billets) bitte	Tickets, please
far'-kart-en (bee'-yay) bitt'-er	
Familienname	Surname
fa-meel'-ee-en-nahm-er	
Fernsprecher	Telephone
fairn'-shprech-er	
Feuerwehr	Fire Brigade
foy'-er-vair	

Frei Free, Vacant
fry

Fundbüro Lost Property Office
foont'-bü-ro

Genaue Adresse Precise address
ger-now'-er a-dress'-er

Gepäckbahnsteig. Nicht aus- Luggage platform. Do not
steigen alight
ger-peck'-bahn-shtīg. nicht owce'-shtīgen

Gift Poison
gift

Hauptbahnhof Main station
howpt'-bahn-hofe

Heben Lift, raise
hay'-ben

Herren Gentlemen
hair'-en

Hinten einsteigen Enter at the rear (on trams,
etc.)
hin'-ten ine'-shtī-gen

Kalt (K) Cold
kult

Kein Ausgang (Durchgang, No Exit (thoroughfare, en-
Eingang) trance)
kine owce'-gung (döörch'-gung, ine'-gung)

Klopfen Knock
klopf'-fen

Krankenhaus. Krankenwagen Hospital. Ambulance
krunk'-en-house, krunk'-en-vahg-en

Langsam fahren Drive slowly
lung'-zum far'-ren

Mit Zuschlag With supplementary charge
mit tsoo'-shlahg

Nachmittags geschlossen Closed in the afternoon
naCH'-mitt-ahgs ger-shloss'-en

Nicht hinauslehnen — Do not lean out
nicht hin-owce'-lay-nen

Nicht parken — No parking
nicht park'-en

Nicht rauchen (Raucher) — No smoking (non-smoker)
nicht rowCH'-en (rowCH'-er)

Notausgang — Emergency exit
note'-owce-gung

Notbremse — Communication cord
note'-brem-zer

Parkplatz — Parking-place
park'-pluts

Personenzug — Stopping train
pair-zone'-en-tsoog

Polizei (-wache) — Police (station)
pol-its-ī (vuCH-er)

Postamt — Post Office
posst'-umt

Rauchen verboten — No smoking
rowCH'-en fair-boat'-en

Rechts fahren — Keep to the right
rechts fa'-ren

Reiseandenken — Souvenirs
rī'-zer-un'-denk-en

Reisebüro — Travel agency
rī'-zer-bü-ro

Schnellzug — Express train
shnell'-tsoog

Strengstens verboten — Strictly forbidden
shtreng'-stens fair-boat'en

Trinkwasser — Drinking water
trink'-vuss-er

Umleitung — Diversion
ōōm'-lī-tōōng

Unterschrift — Signature
ōōn'-ter-shrift

Verbotener Durchgang	No thoroughfare
fair-boat'-en-er dŏŏrch'-gung	

Vorname	Christian name
fore'-nahm-er	

Vorn aussteigen	Alight at the front (of vehicles)
fŏrn owce'-shtī-gen	

Warm (W)	Hot
varm	

Wartesaal (erster, zweiter, dritter Klasse)	Waiting-room (1st, 2nd, 3rd class)
vart'-er-zahl (airst'-er, tsvī'-ter, dritt-er kluss'-er)	

Ziehen	Pull
tsee'-en	

Zollamt	Customs
tsoll'-umt	

GERMAN ABBREVIATIONS

Abf. (Abfahrt), Departure.
B.w. (Bitte wenden), Please turn over.
a/M. (am Main), e.g. Frankfurt am Main.
Ank. (Ankunft), Arrival.
a/O. (an der Oder), Frankfurt an der Oder.
a/Rh. (am Rhein), on the Rhine.
Bayr. (Bayrisch), Bavarian.
Bez. (Bezirk), District.
BP. (Beschleunigter Personenzug), Fast train but not non-stop.
CH. (*Swiss*) (Confederatio Helveticae), used on cars, like "GB".
DM. (D Mark), German Mark (currency).
D-Zug. (Durchgangszug), Through or corridor train.
Eidg. (*Swiss*) (Eidgenössisch), Federal.
Frl. (Fräulein), Miss.
geb. (geboren), born.
Gebr. (Gebrüder), Brothers.
HBF. (Hauptbahnhof), Main station.
i. (in), "in", e.g. Hagen i.W.=Hagen in Westphalia.
JH. (Jugendherberge), Youth Hostel.

kg. (Kilogramm), Kilogramme.

km. (Kilometer), Kilometre.

MEZ. (Mitteleuropäische Zeit), Central European Time (one hour ahead of Greenwich Mean Time).

möbl. (möbliert), furnished.

Nachf. (Nachfolger), Successor.

N. (Norden), North.

NO. (Nordosten), North-East.

NW. (Nordwesten), North-West.

O. (Osten), East.

p.A. (per Adresse), Care of, C/o.

Pf. (Pfennig), One-hundredth part of the D Mark.

Pfd. (Pfund), Pound.

PS. (Pferdestärke), Horse power, h.p.

qm. (Quadratmeter), Square metre.

Reg.Bez. (Regierungsbezirk), Administrative district.

Rh. (Rhein), Rhine.

Rp. (*Swiss*) (Rappen), centime (one-hundredth part of Swiss franc).

S. (Süden), South.

SBB. (*Swiss*) (Schweizerische Bundesbahnen), Swiss Federal Railways.

Str. (Strasse), Street.

u. (und), and.

u.A.w.g. (um Antwort wird gebeten), A reply is requested R.S.V.P.

v. (von), of, from.

vorm. (vormals), formerly; vormittags, before noon, a.m.

W. (Westen), West.

WEZ. (Westeuropäische Zeit), Western European Time (Greenwich Mean Time).

z. (zu), to.

z.B. (zum Beispiel), for example, e.g.

TIME

VOCABULARY

afternoon, der Nachmittag (naCH'-mitt-ahg)
always, immer (imm'-er)
at once, sofort (zo-fort)
beginning, der Anfang (un-fung)
calendar, der Kalender (kah-len'-der)
clock, die Uhr (oor)
day, der Tag (tahg)
daily, täglich (tay'-glich)
during, während (vay-rend)
early, früh (frü)
end, das Ende (end'-er)
evening, der Abend (ah'-bent)
first, zuerst (tsoo-airst)
fortnight, vierzehn Tage (fear'-tsain tahg-er)
hour, die Stunde (shtoond'-er)
last, zuletzt (tsoo-letst')
late, spät (spait)
midday, Mittag (mitt'-ahg)
middle, die Mitte (mitt'-er)
midnight, Mitternacht (mitt'-er-naCHt)
month, der Monat (mō'-naht)
morning, der Morgen (mor'-gen)
never, nie, niemals (nee, nee-mahls)
next, nächst (naich-st)
night, die Nacht (naCHt)
now, jetzt (yetst)
often, oft (oft')
sometimes, manchmal (munch-mahl)
soon, bald (bullt)
then, dann (dunn)
time, die Zeit (tsīte)
today, heute (hoyt'-er)
tomorrow, morgen (mor'-gen)
week, die Woche (voCH'-er)
wristwatch, die Armbanduhr (ahrm-bunt-oor)
year, das Jahr (yahr')
yesterday, gestern (guesst'-ern)

CLOCK TIME

Central European Time.—German, Austrian and Swiss time is one hour ahead of Greenwich Mean Time, i.e. noon in Britain is 1 p.m. in Germany. During British Summer Time the hours are equal, as in Germany the clock is not put forward.

What time is it ?	Wie spät ist es?
	vee shpate ist ez
It is one o'clock	Es ist ein Uhr
	ez ist ine oor
Ten o'clock	Zehn Uhr
	tsain oor
Quarter past ten	Viertel nach zehn
	fear'-tel naCH tsain
Half-past ten	Halb elf (that is, half before 11)
	hulp elf
Quarter to eleven	Viertel vor elf
	fear'-tel fore elf
Eleven a.m.	Elf Uhr morgens
	elf oor morg'-enz
Eleven p.m.	Elf Uhr abends
	elf oor ah'-bents
Twenty past six	Zwanzig nach sechs
	tsvunts'-ich naCH zex
My watch is fast (slow)	Meine Uhr geht vor (geht nach)
	mi'-ner oor gate fore (gate naCH)
Is that clock right ?	Geht diese Uhr richtig?
	gait dee'-zer oor richt'-ich
It is late	Es ist spät
	ez ist shpate
It is still very early	Es ist noch sehr früh
	ez ist noCH zair frü

You have plenty of time	Sie haben viel Zeit
	zee hah-ben feel tsite
Take your time	Nehmen Sie sich Zeit
	nay-men zee sich tsite
We are in a hurry	Wir haben es eilig
	vere hah-ben ez i'-lich
Hurry up!	Machen Sie schnell!
	maCH'-en zee shnell
He is early	Er ist früh
	air ist frü'
He is late	Er hat sich verspätet
	air hat zich fair'-shpate'-et
How long does it take to . . . ?	Wie lange braucht man nach . . . ?
	vee lung-er browCHt mun naCH . . . ?

DAYS OF THE WEEK

Sunday, Sonntag (zonn'-tahg)
Monday, Montag (moan'-tahg)
Tuesday, Dienstag (deenst'-tahg)
Wednesday, Mittwoch (mitt'-voCH)
Thursday, Donnerstag (donn'-ers-tahg)
Friday, Freitag (fry'-tahg)
Saturday, Sonnabend, or Samstag (zonn-ah'-bent, zums'-tahg)
N.B. *All the days of the week are masculine.*
During the day, Tagsüber (tahgs-üb'-er)
At night, nachts (naCHts)
This evening, heute abend (hoy'-ter ah'-bent)
to-day, heute (hoy'-ter)
All day. The next day, Den ganzen Tag (dane gunt'-sen tahg). Der nächste
   Tag (dair next'-er tahg)
A week ago, Vor einer Woche (for i'-ner voCH'-er)

Day before yesterday	Vorgestern
	fore'-guess-tern
Yesterday evening	Gestern Abend
	guess'-tern ah'-bent
Tomorrow morning	Morgen früh
	morg'-en frü

Day after tomorrow	Übermorgen
	ü'-ber-morg-en
For some days past	Seit einigen Tagen
	zite i'-nig-en tahg'-en
Every day	Jeden Tag
	yay'-den tahg
Last week	Vorige Woche
	for'-i'-ger vo'-CHer
Next week	Nächste Woche
	next'-er vo'-CHer
A fortnight on Monday	Montag in vierzehn Tagen
	moan-tahg in fear'-tsain tahg'-en
Holiday	Der Feiertag
	dair fī'-er-tahg
Easter	Ostern
	o'-stern
Whitsuntide	Pfingsten
	pfing'-sten
Christmas	Weihnachten
	vī'-naCHt-en
New Years Day	Neujahr
	noy-yar

MONTHS AND SEASONS

January, Januar (yan'-oo-ar)
February, Februar (faib'-roo-ar)
March, März (mairts)
April, April (up-ril')
May, Mai (my)
June, Juni (yoon'-ee)
July, Juli (yool'-ee)
August, August (ow-goost')
September, September (zep-tem'-ber)
October, Oktober (oc-tō'-ber)
November, November (no-vem'-ber)
December, Dezember (day-tsem'-ber)

Spring, Frühling (frü'-ling)
Summer, Sommer (zomm'-er)
Autumn, Herbst (hairbst)
Winter, Winter (vinter)

On the first of the month   Am Ersten des Monats

um airst-en dez mō´-nahts

April 1st   Der erste April

dair airst-er up-ril´

RESTAURANTS AND CAFÉS

The Café is very popular in Germany, and provides a convenient meeting-place for friends or for the discussion of business. Most restaurants and cafés open early and close late at night. Newspapers and magazines are provided for the use of the customer, and one need not, as in this country, feel obliged to leave as soon as one has consumed one's refreshment.

VOCABULARY

ash-tray, der Aschenbecher (ah-shen-be´-cher)
bar, die Bar (bar)
bill, die Rechnung (rech´-nŏong)
bottle, die Flasche (flush´-er)
bowl, die Schüssel (shüss´-el)
breakfast, das Frühstück (frü´-shtük)
coffee-pot, die Kaffeekanne (kuff´-ay-kun´-er)
cold, kalt (kult)
cork, der Korken (kork´-en)
cork-screw, der Korkenzieher (kork´-en-tsee´-er)
cup (tea, coffee), die Tasse (Teetasse, Kaffeetasse) (tuss´-er) (tay´-tuss´-er, kuff´-ay-tuss´-er)
dessert, der Nachtisch (naCH´-tish)
dinner, das Abendessen (ah´-bent-ess-en)
dish, das Gericht (ger´-icht)
egg-cup, der Eierbecher (ī-er-bech´-er)
fork, die Gabel (gah´-bel)
glass, das Glas (gluss)
hors d'œuvres, die Vorspeise (fore´-shp-īzer)
knife, das Messer (mess´-er)
lunch, das Mittagessen (mit´-ahg-ess-en)
meal, die Mahlzeit (mahl-tsite)
menu, die Speisekarte (shp´ī-zer-kart-er)
milk-jug, der Milchtopf (milch-topf)
napkin, die Serviette (zer-vee-ett´-er)
plate, soup-plate, der Teller, Suppenteller (tell´-er, zŏop´-en-tell´-er)
saucer, die Untertasse (ŏon´-ter-tuss´-er)
snack, der Imbiss (im´-biss)
spoon, table (tea), der Esslöffel (Teelöffel) (ess´-lurf-el, tay´-lurf-el)
supper, das Abendbrot (ah´-bent-broat)
table, table-cloth, der Tisch, das Tischtuch (tish, tish´-tooCH)
tea-pot, die Teekanne (tay´-kunn-er)

tip, das Trinkgeld (trink-gelt)
tooth-pick, der Zahnstocher (tsahn-shtoCH'-er)
waiter, der Ober, Kellner (o'-ber, kell'-ner)
waiter (head), der Oberkellner (o'-ber-kell'-ner)
waitress, die Kellnerin (kell-ner-in)
warm, warm (varm)
water-jug, der Wasserkrug (vuss'-er-kroog)
wine-list, die Weinkarte (vine-kart-er)

DRINKS

alcohol, Alkohol (al'-coh-hol)
beer (light, dark), das Bier (hell, dunkel) (beer, hell, dōōn'-kel)
brandy, der Cognac (con'-yac)
burgundy, der Burgunder (bōōr'-gōōn'-der)
chocolate, die Schokolade (shock-o-lahd'-er)
cider, der Apfelwein (up'-fel-vine)
coffee, der Kaffee (kuff'-ay)
gin, Gin (jin)
hock, der (weisse) Rheinwein (vice'-er rine-vine)
juice (apple, grape, raspberry), der Saft (Apfel, Trauben, Himbeer) (zaft, up'fel, trow-ben, him'-bair)
lager, Das Lagerbier (lah'-ger-beer)
lemonade, die Limonade (lee-mon-ahd'-er)
liqueur, der Likör (leek-urr')
milk, die Milch (milch)
mineral water, das Mineralwasser (min-er-ahl'-vuss-er)
port, der Portwein (port-vine)
rum, der Rum (rōōm)
sherry, der Sherry (sherry)
soda-water, das Selterwasser (zel'-ter-vuss'-er)
water, das Wasser (vuss'-er)
whisky, der Whisky
wine, red, white, der Wein, Rotwein, Weisswein (vine, rote'vine, vice'-vine)

FOOD

apple, der Apfel (up'-fel)
apricot, die Aprikose (ap-ri-kos'-er)
asparagus, der Spargel (shpar'-gel)
bacon (fried bacon), der Speck (gebratener Speck) shpeck (ge-braht'-en-er shpeck)
banana, die Banane (ba-nan-er)
beans (French, white), die Bohnen (grüne, weisse) bo'-nen (grü'-ner, vice'-er)
beef, das Rindfleisch (rint'-flīsh)
biscuit, der Keks (cakes)
bread (white, brown), das Weissbrot, Schwarzbrot (vice-broat, shvar'-ts-broat)
broth, die Fleischbrühe (flīsh'-brü'-er)

butter, die Butter (bŏŏt'-er)
cabbage (white, red), der Weisskohl, Rotkohl (vice'-coal, rote-coal)
cake, der Kuchen (kooCH'-en)
fancy cake (in Switzerland), die Patisserie (pa-teess'-er-ee')
carrots, die Möhren, Karrotten (mur'-ren, kar-ott'-en)
carp, der Karpfen (karrp-fen)
cauliflower, der Blumenkohl (bloo'-men-coal)
celery, die Sellerie (zell'-er-ee)
cheese, der Käse (kay'-zer)
chicken, das Huhn (hoon)
chop, cutlet, das Kotelett (cot-lett)
cod, der Kabeljau (kah'-bel-yow)
crayfish, der Krebs (krayps)
cream, die Sahne (zahn'-er)
cucumber, (salad), die Gurke, der Gurkensalat (goor'-ker, goor'-ken-zul-aht)
doughnut, der Pfannkuchen (pfun'-kooCH'-en)
duck, die Ente (ent'-er)
dumplings, die Klösse (kluss'-er)
egg(s) (soft, hard boiled), weich (hart), gekochte(s), Ei(er) vīch (hart), ger-koCH'-te(z) ī'(-er)
egg, fried, scrambled, Spiegelei, Rührei (shpee'-gel-ī, rür'-ī)
fish, der Fisch (fish)
fruit, das Obst (ōbst)
fruit tart, die Obsttorte (ōbst'-tort-er)
game, das Wild (vilt)
garlic, der Knoblauch (knōb-lowCH)
grapes, die Weintrauben (vine'-trow-ben)
gravy, die Sosse (zōss-er)
ham, raw, boiled, der Schinken, roh, gekochter (shink'-en, ro, ger-koCHt-er)
herring, der Hering (hair'-ing)
haddock, der Schellfisch (shell'fish)
hake, der Hecht (hecht)
halibut, der Heilbutt (hile'-boot)
ice, ice-cream, das Eis (ice)
jam, die Marmelade (mar-mel-ahd'er)
kidney, die Niere (neer'-er)
lamb, das Lammfleisch (lumm'-flīsh)
liver, die Leber (lay'-ber)
lemon, die Zitrone (tsee-trō'-ner)
leek, das Lauch (lowCH)
lettuce, der Kopfsalat (kopf'-zul-aht')
lobster, der Hummer (hŏŏm'-er)
marmalade, die Orangenmarmelade (o-rong'-jen-mar-mel-ahd'-er)
meat (cold), der Aufschnitt (owf-shnitt)
melon, die Melone (may-loan'-er)
mushrooms, die Pilze (pilts-er)
mussels, die Muscheln (mŏŏsh-eln)
mutton, das Hammelfleisch (humm'-el-flīsh)
mustard, der Senf (zenf)

oil, das Öl (url)
omelette, das Omelett (om-lett′)
onion, die Zwiebel (tsvee′-bel)
orange, die Apfelsine (up-fel-zee′-ner)
oysters, die Austern (owce′-tern)
oxtail, der Ochsenschwanz (ox′-sen-shvants)
partridge, das Rebhuhn (rape′-hoon)
pastry, der Teig (tīg)
peach, der Pfirsich (pfeer′-zich)
pear, die Birne (beer′-ner)
peas, Erbsen (airb′-zen)
pepper, der Pfeffer (pfeff′-er)
pheasant, der Fasan (fa-zahn′)
pie, die Pastete (pus-tay′-ter)
pineapple, die Ananas (un′-un-uss)
plaice, die Scholle (sholl′-er)
plum, die Pflaume (pflow′-mer)
plum-tart, der Pflaumenkuchen (pflow′-men-koo-CHen)
pork, das Schweinefleisch (shvine′-er-flīsh)
potatoes (fried), die Kartoffeln (Bratkartoffeln) kar-toff′-eln (braht′-kar-toff′-eln)
poultry, das Geflügel (ger-flü′-gel)
pudding, der Pudding (pudding)
rabbit, das Kaninchen (kun-een′-chen)
radish, das Radieschen (ra-deess′-chen)
raspberry, die Himbeere (him′-bair-er)
rhubarb, der Rhabarber (ra-barb′-er)
rice, der Reis (rice)
roll, das Brötchen (brurt′-chen)
salad, der Salat (zul-aht′)
salami, die Salami (salami)
salmon, der Lachs (lucks)
salt, das Salz (zults)
sardines (in oil), die Ölsardinen (url′-zar-deen′-nen)
sandwich, das belegte Brot (bel-ayg′-ter broat)
sauce, die Sosse (zoss′-er)
sausage, die Wurst (voorst)
shrimps, die Krabben (krab′-en)
sole, die Seezunge (zay-tsoong′-er)
soup, gravy, die Suppe, die Kraftbrühe (zoop-′er, kruft′-brü-er)
soup, clear (thick), die Bouillon, Suppe mit Einlage (boo-yong′, zoop′-er mit ine′-lahge)
spinach, der Spinat (shpee-naht′)
steak, das Schnitzel (shnit-sel)
stewed fruit, das Kompott (kom-pot′)
strawberries, die Erdbeeren (airt′-bair-en)
sugar, der Zucker (tsook′-er)
sweets, Süssigkeiten, Pralinen (züss′-ich-kite-en, prahl′-een-ay)
toast, der Toast (toast)
tongue, die Zunge (tsoong′-er)

tomato, die Tomate (to-maht'-er)
trout, die Forelle (for-ell'-er)
turkey, der Truthahn (troot'-hahn)
turnip, die Kohlrübe (coal-rü-ber)
veal, das Kalbfleisch (kulp-flīsh)
vegetable, das Gemüse (ger-mü-zer)
vegetable marrow, der Kürbis (kür-biss)
venison, das Wildbret (vilt-bret)
vinegar, der Essig (ess'-ich)

Can I lunch (dine) here ?	Kann man hier zu Mittag (Abend) essen?
	kun mun here tsoo mitt'-ahg (ah'-bent) ess-en
We would like a table for four	Wir möchten einen Tisch für vier Personen
	vere murch'-ten ī-nen tish für feer pair-zō'-nen
Can I have a table near the window ?	Kann ich einen Tisch am Fenster haben?
	kun ich ī'-nen tish um fen'-ster hah'-ben
Waiter !	Herr Ober!
	hair ō'-ber!
Waitress !	Kellnerin !
	kell'-ner-in
Where can I have a wash ?	Wo kann ich mich waschen?
	vo kun ich mich vush'-en
Between what times is dinner served ?	Um welche Zeit wird das Abendessen serviert?
	oom velch'-er tsīte virt duss ah'-bent-ess-en sair-veert
Have you a set menu for lunch?	Haben Sie ein Tagesgericht?
	hah'-ben zee ine tahg'-es-ger'-icht
We don't want a complete meal	Wir möchten keine volle Mahlzeit
	vere murcht'-en kīn'-er foll'-er mahl-tsīte
We shall come back in an hour	Wir werden in einer Stunde wiederkommen
	vere verd'-en in ī'-ner shtōōnd'-er vee'-der-komm'-en
Bring me the menu (wine-list) please	Bringen Sie mir bitte die Speisekarte (Weinkarte)
	bring'-en zee mere bitt'-er dee shpī'-zer-kart-er (vine'-kart-er)

Which dish do you recommend ?   Welches Gericht empfehlen Sie?

vell'-ches ger'-icht emp-fay'-len zee

We want only a snack   Wir möchten nur einen Imbiss

vere murch'-ten noor i'-nen im-biss

Please serve us quickly, we are in a hurry   Bitte bedienen Sie uns schnell, wir haben es eilig

bitt-er bed-een'-en zee oons shnell, vere hah'-ben ez ī-lich

I am hungry (thirsty)   Ich habe Hunger (Durst)

ich hah'-ber hoong'-er (doorst)

What kind of soup have you?   Was für Suppe haben Sie?

vuss für zoop'-er hah'-ben zee

I will have some fried fish   Ich möchte gebratenen Fisch

ich murcht'-er geb-raht-e-nen fish

Then we will take roast meat and vegetables   Dann nehmen wir Fleischbraten und Gemüse

dunn nay'-men vere flish-braht'-en oont ger mü'-zer

Can we have steak and chips ?   Können wir Schnitzel und pommes frites haben?

kurn'-en vere shnits'-el oont pawm freet hah-ben

Would you like a sweet or some fruit?   Möchten Sie Nachtisch oder etwas Obst?

murcht'-en zee naCH-tish ō'-dair et'-vuss ōbst

Give us a light (brown) ale please   Bringen Sie uns ein helles (dunkles) Bier bitte

bring'-en zee ōons ine hell'-es (doonk-les) beer bitt'-er

I would like something refreshing   Ich möchte etwas Erfrischendes

ich murcht'-er et'-vuss air-frish-end-es

We would like black coffee (white coffee, coffee with cream)   Wir möchten schwarzen Kaffee (Milchkaffee, Kaffee mit Sahne)

vere murcht'-en shvarts'-en kuff'-ay (milch-kuff'-ay, kuff'-ay mit zahn'-er)

Can you recommend a good (cheap) local wine ?   Können Sie einen guten (billigen) Wein aus der Umgegend empfehlen

kurn'-en zee i-nen goot'-en (hill-ig-en) vine owce dair ōōm'-gayg-ent emp-fay'-len

I like it underdone (well done)   Ich möchte es halbgebraten
(gut gebraten)

ich murch'-ter ez hulp'-geb-raht-en, goot geb-raht-en

Bring us two rolls each and some butter, please   Bringen Sie uns bitte je zwei
Brötchen und Butter

bring'-en zee ōōns bitt'-er yay tsvi brurt'-chen ōōnt bōōt-er

Tea (with rum, lemon, milk) for one and coffee for three   Einmal Tee (mit Rum, Zitrone,
Milch) und drei Kaffee

ine'-mahl tay (mit rōōm, tsee-tro'-ner, milch) ōōnt dry kuff'-ay

Please call the head waiter   Bitte, rufen Sie den Oberkellner

bitt'-er roof'-en zee dane ō-ber-kell-ner

The food is cold   Das Essen ist kalt

duss ess'-en ist kult

This is not properly cooked   Das ist nicht richtig gekocht

duss ist nicht rich'-tich ger-koCHt

Bring me another helping   Geben Sie mir noch eine
Portion

gay'-ben zee mere noCH i'-ner por-tsee-ōn

No, thank you, I have had enough   Danke, ich habe genug gehabt

dunk'-er, ich hah'-ber ger-nōōCH ger-hubt'

Yes, please   Ja, bitte

yah, bitt'-er

Bring me another knife (fork, spoon, plate)   Bringen Sie mir noch ein
Messer (eine Gabel, einen
Löffel, einen Teller)

bring'-en zee mere noCH ine mess'-er (i'-ner gahb'-el, i'-nen lurf'-el, i'-nen tell-er)

A glass of iced water, please   Ein Glas Eiswasser bitte

ine gluss ice'-vuss-er bitt'-er

Bill, please   Zahlen bitte

tsah'-len bitt'-er

Is that with service included?   Ist die Bedienung einbegriffen?

ist dee bed-een'-ōōng ine'-beg-riff-en

Pay at the desk   An der Kasse zahlen

un dair kuss'-er tsah'-len

Keep the change	Das stimmt so
	duss shtimmt zo
I have already paid for the service	Ich habe bereits für die Bedienung bezahlt
	ich hah'-ber ber'-īts für dee bed-een'-ōong ber-tsahlt
There is a mistake in the bill	Die Rechnung ist nicht in Ordnung
	dee rech'-nōong ist nicht in ord'-nōong
Check it please	Rechnen Sie es bitte nach
	rech'-nen zee es bitt'-er naCH
I made a mistake. I beg your pardon	Ich habe mich geirrt. Entschuldigen Sie bitte
	ich hah'-ber mich ger'-irrt. ent-shōōl-dig-en zee bitt'-er

GENERAL DIFFICULTIES

I want to eat something very simple	Ich möchte etwas Einfaches essen
	ich murcht'-er et'-vuss īne-faCH'-es ess-en
I am on a diet	Ich muss Diät essen
	ich mōōss dee-ate ess'-en
The wine is corked	Korken ist im Wein
	kork'-en ist im vine
This is not very fresh	Das ist nicht frisch
	duss ist nicht frish
This piece is fat	Dieses Stück ist zu fett
	dee-zes shtück ist tsoo fet
Give me a lean piece please	Bringen Sie mir bitte ein mageres Stück
	bring'-en zee mere bitt'-er ine mahg'-er-es shtück
While I was dining someone has taken my . . .	Als ich speiste hat jemand mein . . . gestohlen
	ulss ich shpīst'-er hat yay'-munt mine . . . ger-shtohl-en

I have left my glasses (my watch, a ring) in the toilet	Ich habe meine Brille (meine Uhr, einen Ring) in der Toilette gelassen

ich hah'-ber mī-ner brill'-er (mī'-ner oor, i'-nen ring) in dair twa-lett'-er ger-lass'-en

MOTORING

Information on taking a car abroad should be obtained from either the Automobile Association or the Royal Automobile Club, who can provide the necessary papers and arrange for customs facilities. Throughout Germany, Austria and Switzerland cars drive on the right side of the road and overtake on the left. Petrol is sold by the litre (Liter, pronounced leet'-er); one gallon equals about 4½ litres. Distances and speed are measured in kilometres (Kilometer—keel'-o-may-ter).

Current regulations regarding speed limits, lighting-up times and so on should be ascertained at the start of the journey.

VOCABULARY

ROAD SIGNS

beware of tar, Vorsicht Teer (for'-sicht tair)
school, Schule (shool'-er)
pedestrian crossing, Fussgänger Übergang (fooss'-geng-er ü-ber-gung)
roadworks ahead, Strassenarbeiten (shtrahss'-en-ar-bite'-en)
road junction, Kreuzung (kroy'-tsoong)
uneven road, unebene Strasse (ōōn-ay-ber'-ner shtrass'-er)
surface damaged by frost, Strassenoberfläche durch Frost beschädigt (shtrass'-en-ō'-ber-flech'-er dōōrch frost ber'-shed'-igt)
overtaking prohibited, Überholen verboten (ü'-ber-ho-len fair-boat'-en)
running in, Einfahren (ine'-fahr-en)
beware of flying stones, Rollsplitt (roll-shplitt)
hospital, Krankenhaus (krunk'-en-house)
level crossing, Bahnübergang (bahn-ü'-ber-gung)
steep hill, steiler Hügel (shty'-ler hü'-gel)
cycle track, Radfahrweg (rahd-fahr'-vayg)
heavy traffic (lorries), Schwere Lastkraftfahrzeuge (shvair'-er lust-kraft-fahr-tsoyg'-er)
slow, langsam (lung'-zahm)
roundabout, Rundell (rōōnd'-ell)
narrow road, enge Strasse (eng'-er shtrasse'-er)
slippery surface in damp weather, Rutschgefahr (rōōtsh'-ger'-fahr)
winding road, kurvenreiche Strasse (koor-ven-rīch'-er shtrass'-er)
road blocked, Strasse gesperrt (strahss'-er ger'-shperrt)
no entry, keine Einfahrt (kī'-ner ine'-fahrt)
one way street, Einbahnstrasse (ine'-bahn-shtrahss-er)

factory exit (lorry exit), Fabrikausfahrt (Ausfahrt für Lastwagen) fah'-
 breek-owce'-fahrt (owce'-fahrt für lust'-wah'-gen)
parking allowed, Parken gestattet (park'-en ger'-shtatt'-et)
parking prohibited (compulsory) on even (odd) days, Parken verboten
 (obligatorisch) an geraden (ungeraden) Tagen park'-en fair'-boat'-en
 (ob'-lee-gah-toe-rish) un ger'-ah'-den (ōōn'-ger-ah'-den) tahg'-en
parking limited to 30 minutes, Parken auf dreissig Minuten beschränkt
 (park'-en owf dry'-sich mee-noot'-en ber'-shrenkt)

GENERAL

air, die Luft (lōōft)
breakdown, die Panne (punn'-er)
breakdown truck, der Abschleppwagen (up-shlepp-vah-gen)
bend, die Kurve (koor'-ver)
caravan, der Wohnwagen (vohn-vah-gen)
car-ferry, die Autofähre (ow'-to-fair-er)
car licence, die Kraftfahrzeuggenehmigung (kraft'-fahr-tsoyg-ger'-nay-
 mee-gōōng)
convertible, das Coupé (koo'-pay)
cross roads, die Kreuzung (kroy-tsōōng)
cyclist, der Radfahrer (raht'-far-er)
diversion, die Umleitung (ōōm'-light-ōōng)
drive, to, fahren (fahr-en)
driver, der Fahrer (fahr-er)
driving licence, der Führerschein (für'-er-shine)
fine, die Strafe (shtrahf-er)
garage, die Garage (gar-age')
highway code, die Verkehrsregel (fair-kairz-ray-gel)
lorry, der Lastwagen (lust'-vahg-en)
maximum speed, die Höchstgeschwindigkeit (hurkst'-gesh-vin-dich-kite)
mechanic, der Autoschlosser (ow'-to-shloss-er)
motorway, die Autobahn (ow-to-bahn)
oil, das Öl (url)
parking-place, der Parkplatz (park'-pluts)
pedestrian, der Fussgänger (fooss'-geng-er)
petrol station, die Tankstelle (tunk'-shtell-er)
repairs, die Reparatur (rep-ahr-aht-oor)
road map, die Strassenkarte (shtrass-en-kart'-er)
road sign, das Verkehrszeichen (fair-kairz'-tsī-chen)
saloon, die Limousine (lee'-moo-see'-ner)
speed limit, die Geschwindigkeitsgrenze (gesh-vin-dich-kites-grents'-er)
skid, to, rutschen (rōōtsh-en)
snow chains, die Schneeketten (shnai-kett'-en)
traffic jam, die Verkehrsstockung (fair-kairz-stock'-ōōng)
traffic lights, die Verkehrsampel (fair-kairz-ump'-el)
traffic policeman, der Verkehrspolizist (fair-kairz-pol-it-sist)
trailer, der Anhänger (un'-heng'-er)
two-stroke mixture, die Zweitackt Mischung (tsvī-tahkt mish-ōōng)

CAR

axle (front, rear), die (Vorder-, Hinter-) Achse (ford'-er, hint'-er ak-ser)
battery, die Batterie (ba-ter-ree)
body, die Karosserie (kar'-ross-er-ee)
bolt, der Bolzen (boll'-tsen)
bonnet, die Motorhaube (mo-tor-how-ber)
boot, der Kofferraum (koff-er-rowm)
brake (drum, pedal), die Bremse, (die Bremstrommel, das Bremspedal) (bremz'-er, bremz-trom-mel, bremz-peh-dahl)
brake lining, der Bremsbelag (bremz'-ber-lahg)
bulb, die Birne (beer'-ner)
bumper, die Stossstange (shtoess-shtahng-er)
car, das Auto (ow'-to)
disc brake, die Scheibenbremse (shy'-ben-brem'-zer)
door, die Tür (tür)
dynamo, die Lichtmaschine (licht-ma-sheen-er)
file, die Feile (fïl-er)
funnel, der Trichter (tricht'-er)
grease gun, die Fettpresse (fet-press-er)
hammer, der Hammer (humm-er)
hand brake, die Handbremse (hunt'-bremz'-er)
head lamps, die Scheinwerfer (shine-ver-fer)
hood, das Verdeck (fair'-deck)
hub cap, die Radkappe (raht'-cup-er)
horn, die Hupe (hoop'-er)
ignition, die Zündung (tsünd-ōōng)
ignition key, der Starterschlüssel (start'-er-shlüss'-el)
indicator, der Winker (vink-er)
inner tube, der Luftschlauch (lōōft'-shlowCH)
jack, der Wagenheber (vah-gen-hayb'-er)
lever, der Hebel (hay'-bel)
lights, die Scheinwerfer (shine'-vairf'-er)
mirror, der Spiegel (shpee'-gel)
number plate, das Nummernschild (nōōm-ern-shilt)
nut, die Schraubenmutter (shrow-ben-mōōt'-er)
oil pressure gauge, der Öldruckmesser (url-drōōk-mess-er)
petrol gauge, die Benzinuhr (ben-tseen'-oor)
petrol tank, der Benzintank (ben-tseen'-tunk)
pliers, die Zange (tsung-er)
propeller shaft, die Antriebswelle (un'-treebs'-vell'-er)
radiator, der Kühler (kühl-er)
rear light, das Rücklicht (rück-licht)
reverse, to, rückwärts fahren (rück'-vairts fahr'-en)
rim (of wheel), die Felge (fell'-ger)
screw, to, schrauben (shrow'-ben)
screw, die Schraube (shrowb'-er)
screwdriver, der Schraubenzieher (shrowb-en-tsee'-er)
self starter, der Anlasser (un-luss-er)
shock absorber, der Stossdämpfer (shtoss-demp-fer)

side lights, die Kotflügellampen (coat-flü-gel-lump-en)
socket wrench, der Steckschlüssel (shteck-shlüss-el)
spanner, der Schraubenschlüssel (shrowb-en-schlüss-el)
spare wheel, das Reserverad (ray-serve-rahd)
speedometer, der Geschwindigkeitsmesser (gesh-vin-dich-kites-mess-er)
spotlight, das Suchlicht (sooCH-licht)
spring, die Feder (fay'-der)
steering wheel, das Steuerrad (shtoy'-er-raht)
tank, der Tank (tunk)
tappet, der Stössel (shturss'-el)
transmission, das Getriebe (*ger'-tree'-ber*)
tyre, der Reifen (rī'-fen)
tyre lever, der Montagehebel (mon-ta-ge-hay-bel)
tyre pump, die Luftpumpe (looft-poomp-er)
universal joint, das Kreuzgelenk (kroyts-gay-lenk)
unscrew, to, abschrauben (up-shrow'-ben)
washer, der Dichtungsring (dich'-toongs-ring)
wheel, front, rear, das Vorder-, Hinterrad (ford-er-, hint-er-raht)
window, das Fenster (fen'-ster)
windscreen, die Windschutzscheibe (vind-shōōts-shī-ber)
windscreen wipers, die Scheibenwischer (shī-ben-vish-er)

ENGINE

accelerator, der Gashebel (gus-hay-bel)
air filter, der Luftfilter (looft-filter)
big end, das Endlager (ent'-lahg'-er)
camshaft, die Nockenwelle (nok-ken-vell-er)
carburettor, der Vergaser (fair-gahz'-er)
choke, der Luftregulierknopf (lōōft'-ray-goo-leer-knopf)
clutch, clutch pedal, die Kupplung, Kupplungshebel (kōōp'-lōōng, kōōp'-lōōngs-hay-bel)
crank-case, das Kurbelgehäuse (koor'-bel-ger'-hoy'-zer)
crank-shaft, die Kurbelwelle (kōōr-bel-vell-er)
cylinder, der Zylinder (tsee'-lind'-er)
distributor, der Verteiler (fair-tīl-er)
engine, der Motor (mo'-tōr)
exhaust pipe, das Auspuffrohr (ows-poof-roar)
fan, der Ventilator (van-tea-lah-tor)
fan belt, der Keilriemen (kīl-ree'-men)
gear box, der Getriebekasten (ger-treeb'-er-kust-en)
gear, der Gang (gung)
gear lever, der Schalthebel (shult'-hay-bel)
oil filter, der Ölfilter (url-filter)
oil pump, die Ölpumpe (url-poomp-er)
piston, der Kolben (kol-ben)
piston rings, die Kolbenringe (kol-ben-ring-er)
sparking plug, die Zündkerze (tsünt'-kairts-er)
starter, der Anlasser (un'-lass'-er)
valve, das Ventil (van-teel)

I do not understand the regulations	Ich verstehe die Verkehrsregeln nicht
	ich fair-shtay'-er dee fair-kairz-ray-geln nicht
Must I fill up a form?	Muss ich ein Formular ausfüllen?
	mŏŏss ich ine for'-moo-lahr owce'-füll'-en
Do you do repairs?	Führen Sie Reparaturen aus?
	fü'-ren zee ray-par-a-toor'-en owce
Is the garage open all night?	Ist die Garage die ganze Nacht offen?
	ist dee gar-agé dee gunts'-er naCHt off'-en
My car (motor-cycle) is two kilometres from here	Mein Wagen (Motorrad) ist zwei Kilometer von hier
	mine vahg'-en (mo-tōr'-raht) ist tsvī keel'-o-mait-er fon here
Can you send a break-down truck?	Können Sie einen Abschleppwagen schicken?
	kurn'-en zee ī'-nen up-shlepp-vahg'-en shick'-en
Please see what is wrong	Bitte sehen Sie nach was es ist
	bitt'-er zay'-en zee naCH vuss ez ist
The engine is overheated	Der Motor ist überhitzt
	dair mo-tōr' ist ü-ber-hitst
It will not start	Der Motor springt nicht an
	dair mo-tōr' shpringt nicht un
Will you repair this puncture?	Können Sie bitte diesen Reifen flicken?
	kurn'-en zee bitt'-er dee'-zen rī'-fen flick'-en
The carburettor needs adjusting	Der Vergaser muss eingestellt werden
	dair fair-gahz'-er mŏŏss ine'-ger-shtellt vaird'-en
You have a blown cylinder gasket	Der Zylinder bläst durch
	dair tsee'-linder blaihst dŏŏrch
Your sparking plugs need cleaning	Die Zündkerzen müssen gereinigt werden
	dee tsunt'-kair-tsen müss'-en ge-rī-nigt vaird'-en

I require new sparking plugs   Ich brauche neue Zündkerzen

ich browCH'-er noy'-er tsünt'-kair-tsen

The engine needs decarbonising   Der Motor muss gereinigt werden

dair mo-tōr' mōōss ge-rī-nigt vaird'-en

The tappets need adjusting   Die Stössel müssen eingestellt werden

dee shturss'-el müss'-en ine'-ger-shtellt vaird'-en

I have had a short-circuit   Ich habe einen Kurzschluss gehabt

ich hah'-ber ī'-nen kōōrts'-shlōōss ger-hubt

I want some petrol (water, oil)   Ich möchte Benzin (Wasser, Öl) haben

ich murch'-ter ben-tseen (vuss'-er, url) hah'-ben

Give me . . . litres, please   Geben Sie mir bitte . . . Liter

gay-ben zee mere bitt-er — leet'-er

I need some more water in the radiator   Ich brauche noch etwas Wasser im Kühler

ich browCH'-er noCH et'-vuss vuss'-er im kü'-ler

I need air in the tyres   Ich brauche Luft in den Reifen

ich browCH'-er lōōft in dane rī'-fen

Will you test the tyre pressure?   Würden Sie bitte den Reifendruck prüfen?

vür-den zee bitt'-er dane rī-fen-drōōck prü'-fen

Top up the battery with distilled water   Die Batterie mit destilliertem Wasser auffüllen

dee but'-te-ree mit des-till-leer-tem vuss'-er owf-fül-len

Are parking lights necessary?   Sind Parklichter erforderlich?

zint park-licht'-er air-ford-air'-lich

I have lost all my documents   Ich habe meine Papiere verloren

ich hah'-ber mī'-ner pup'-eer'-er fair-lō'-ren

I want to hire a car   Ich möchte einen Wagen mieten

ich murch'-ter ī'-nen vahg'-en mee'-ten

How much is it for the day?	Wieviel verlangen Sie für den ganzen Tag?
	vee-feel' fair-lung'-en zee für dane gunts'-en tahg
Do you know the road to . . .?	Kennen Sie den Weg nach . . .?
	kenn'- en zee dane vaig naCH . . .?
We are going to lunch here	Wir werden hier zu Mittag essen
	vere vaird'-en here tsoo mit'-ahg ess'-en
Pick us up at . . .	Holen Sie uns um . . . ab
	hole-en zee ŏŏns ŏŏm . . . up
We must be back by . . .	Wir müssen um . . . zurück sein
	vere müss'-en ŏŏm . . . tsoo-rük' zine
Can I garage my car for the night (a week) ?	Kann ich meinen Wagen für eine Nacht (eine Woche) unterstellen?
	kun ich mi'-nen vahg'-en für i'-ner naCHt (i'-ner voCH'-er) ŏŏnt'-er-shtell-en
Wash and grease the car	Waschen und schmieren Sie den Wagen
	vush'-en ŏŏnt shmeer'-en zee dane vahg'-en
How long will it take ?	Wie lange wird es dauern?
	vee lung'-er virt ez dow'-ern
When can I collect the car ?	Wann kann ich den Wagen abholen?
	vun kun ich dane vahg'-en up'-ho-len
What time does the garage close ?	Um welche Zeit schliesst die Garage?
	ŏŏm vellch'-er tsite shleesst dee gar-agé
Where is the nearest garage for repairs ?	Wo ist die nächste Reparatur-werkstätte?
	vo ist dee next'-er ray-par-a-toor'-vairk-shtett-er
Can you tow me there ?	Können Sie mich dahin ab-schleppen?
	kurn'-en zee mich dah-hin' up-shlepp'-en
This must be replaced (straightened)	Das muss ersetzt (gerade gemacht) werden
	duss mŏŏss air'-zetst (ger'-ahd'-er ger'-maCHt) vaird'-en

There is a rattle I cannot find	Da ist ein Geräusch, das ich nicht finden kann

dah ist ine ger'-oysh, duss ich nicht find'-en kun

There is a leak in the . . .	Der . . . ist undicht

dair . . . ist ŏŏn'-dicht

Can you lend me . . .?	Können Sie mir . . . leihen?

kurn'-en zee mere . . . lei'-en

Start! Stop!	Starten! Anhalten!

start'-en! un'-hal-ten!

Go into second (third, fourth) gear	Schalten Sie den zweiten (dritten, vierten) Gang ein

shult'-en zee dane tsvī'-ten (dritt'-en, fear'-ten) gung ine

I have engine trouble	Ich habe einen Motordefekt

ich hah'-ber i'-nen mo-tōr'-day-fect

The brakes need adjusting	Die Bremsen müssen angezogen werden

dee brem'-zen müss'-en un'-gē-tsu-gen vairΠΙ'-en

Can you please charge the battery?	Können Sie bitte die Batterie aufladen

kurn'-en zee bitt'-er dee but-ter-ree owf-lahd'-en

What will the repairs cost?	Wieviel wird die Reparatur kosten?

vee-feel virt dee ray-par-a-toor kost'-en

TRAVEL

CUSTOMS AND PORTERS

The customs regulations in Germany, Austria and Switzerland are in general the same as in the United Kingdom. Coffee and tea however, may only be imported into Germany free of duty if the traveller is carrying equipment clearly showing his intention to camp.

VOCABULARY

bag, die Tasche (tush'-er)
camera, die Kamera (kum'-er-ah)
cigar, die Zigarre (tsi-gar'-er)
cigarettes, Zigaretten (tsi-gar-ett'-en)

customs, das Zollamt (tsoll'-umt)
customs officer, der Zollbeamte (tsoll'-bay-umt'-er)
declare, to, verzollen (fair-tsol'-en)
examine, to, kontrollieren (kon-trol-eer'-en)
hand luggage, das Handgepäck (hunt'-gep-eck)
hat, der Hut (hoot)
journey, die Reise (rī'-zer)
key, der Schlüssel (shlüss'-el)
label, die Aufschrift (owf'-shrift)
luggage, das Gepäck (gep-eck)
number, die Nummer (noōm'-er)
open, to, aufmachen (owf'-maCH-en)
overcoat, der Mantel (mun'-tel)
parcel, das Paket (puck-ate')
passport, der Pass (pus)
porter, der Gepäckträger (gep-eck-tray'-ger)
raincoat, der Regenmantel (ray'-gen-munt-el)
spirits, die Spirituosen (shpee'-ri-too-oh'-zen)
souvenir, das Reiseandenken (rī'-zer-un-denk-en)
station, der Bahnhof (bahn'-hōf)
suitcase, der Handkoffer (hunt-koff'-er)
tobacco, der Tabak (tah-buk')
train, der Zug (tsoog)
trunk, der Koffer (koff'-er)
umbrella, der Schirm (shirm)

Porter !	Träger !
	tray'-ger
Please take my luggage	Bitte nehmen Sie mein Gepäck
	bitt'-er nay'-men zee mine gep-eck'
I have a lot of luggage	Ich habe viel Gepäck
	ich hah'-ber feel gep-eck'
Four pieces	Vier Stück
	feer shtück
I shall take my hand luggage	Ich nehme mein Handgepäck
	ich nay'mer mine hunt-gep-eck
I only have a suitcase and a bag	Ich habe nur einen Handkoffer und eine Tasche
	ich hah'-ber noor i-nen hunt-koff'-er ŏŏnt i-ner tush'-er
There is one suitcase missing	Es fehlt ein Handkoffer
	ez failt ine hunt'-koff-er
That is mine over there	Das ist meins, da drüben
	duss ist mines, dah drü'-ben

These are not mine	Diese sind nicht meine Sachen

dee-se zint nicht mī'-ner zaCH'-en

I cannot find my porter — Ich kann meinen Träger nicht finden

ich kun mī'-nen tray'-ger nicht fin'-den

Have you seen porter 155? — Haben Sie Träger Nummer Einhundertfünfundfünfzig gesehen?

hah'-ben zee tray'-ger nōōm'-er ine'-hōōn-dert-fünf-ōōnt-fünf'-tsich ger'-zay-en

How much do I owe you? — Was schulde ich Ihnen?

vuss shōōld'-er ich ee'-nen

Where is the Customs? — Wo ist das Zollamt?

vo ist duss tsoll'-umt

Here is my passport — Hier ist mein Pass

here ist mine puss

I have nothing to declare — Ich habe nichts zu verzollen

ich hah'-ber nichts tsoo fair-tsol'-en

They are for my personal use — Sie sind für meinen persönlichen Gebrauch

zee zint für mī'-nen pair-zurn' lich-en geb-rowCH'

Open this suitcase please — Machen Sie bitte diesen Koffer auf

maCH-en zee bitt'-er dee-zen koff-er owf'

I have lost my keys — Ich habe meine Schlüssel verloren

ich hah'-ber mī'-ner shlüss'-el fair-lō'-ren

I cannot open my case — Ich kann meinen Koffer nicht aufmachen

ich kun mī'-nen koff'-er nicht owf'-maCH-en

I have bought a few souvenirs — Ich habe einige Reiseandenken gekauft

ich hah'-ber i-ni-ger rī'-zer-un-denk-en ger-kowft

Are these things dutiable? — Sind diese Sachen verzollbar?

zint dee'-zer zaCH'-en fair-tsol'-bar

Have you finished? — Sind Sie fertig?

zint zee fair'-tich

My luggage has been examined Mein Gepäck ist schon kon-
trolliert

<small>mine gep-eck ist shone kon-trol-eert'</small>

Please mark these Bitte zeichnen Sie diese

<small>bitt'-er tsïch'-nen zee dee-zer</small>

I shall meet you on Platform Ich treffe Sie auf Bahnsteig
Three drei

<small>ich treff'-er zee owf bahn'-shtïg drï</small>

TRAINS

There are two main types of train in Germany; the slow train or *Personenzug* and the express or *Schnellzug, Eilzug.* For travel by express train a
small supplementary charge (*Zuschlag*) is made. This does not apply in
Switzerland. Visitors to Switzerland may find it worth while to take advantage of the reduced rates for rail travel offered under the Holiday
Ticket System.

In Germany seat reservations (*Platzkarten*) may be had at extra charge.
Second-class travel is comfortable.

Where the train has a restaurant car there is more latitude in the times
of serving meals than there is in Britain. Light refreshments and drinks may
be had at any time.

Luggage can be registered for a moderate charge. It is given up at the
station of departure, and the traveller need not have anything more to do
with it till he collects it on arrival at his destination.

VOCABULARY

arrival, die Ankunft (un-koŏnft)
berth, das Bett (bett')
blanket, die Decke (deck'-er)
booking-office, der Fahrkartenschalter (far'-kart-en-shult'-er)
carriage (coach), der Eisenbahnwagen (ï'-zen-bahn-vahg'-en)
communication cord, die Notbremse (note'-brem-zer)
compartment, das Abteil (up'-tile)
connection, der Anschluss (un'-shloŏss)
corridor, der Korridor (kor'-ee-door)
departure, die Abfahrt (up'-fart)
dining-car, der Speisewagen (shpï'-zer-vah-gen)
door, die Tür (tür)
engine, die Lokomotive (lo-ko-mo-tea'-ver)
enquiry office, die Auskunft (owce'-koŏnft)
express train, der Schnellzug (shnell'-tsoog)
guard, der Zugführer (tsoog'-für-er)
journey, die Reise (rï'-zer)

left luggage, die Gepäckaufbewahrung (gep-eck'-owf-ber-vah-roong)
level-crossing, der Bahnübergang (bahn-ü'-ber-gung)
lost property office, das Fundbüro (fŏŏnt'-bü-ro)
luggage-van, der Gepäckwagen (gep-eck-vah-gen)
passenger, der Reisende (rī'-zen-der)
pillow, das Kopfkissen (kopf'-kiss-en)
platform, der Bahnsteig (bahn'-shtīg)
platform ticket, die Bahnsteigkarte (bahn'-shtīg-kart-er)
refreshment room, der Speisesaal (shpī'-zer-zahl)
rack, das Gepäcknetz (gep-eck-nets)
return ticket, die Rückfahrkarte (rük'-far-kart-er)
seat, der Platz (pluts)
seat reservation, die Platzkarte (pluts kart-er)
sleeping-car, der Schlafwagen (shlahf'-vah-gen)
smoking compartment, das Raucherabteil (rowCH'-er up'-tile)
station, der Bahnhof (bahn'-hōf)
stationmaster, der Bahnhofsvorsteher (bahn'-hōfs-fore-shtay-er)
subway, die Unterführung (ŏŏn'-ter-fü-rŏŏng)
supplementary charge, der Zuschlag (tsoo'-shlahg)
ticket, die Fahrkarte (far-kart-er)
time-table, der Fahrplan (far'-plun)
train, der Zug (tsoog)
tunnel, das Tunnel (tŏŏ'-nel)
waiting-room, der Wartesaal (vart'-er-zahl)
window, das Fenster (fen'-ster)

Where is the booking-office ?	Wo ist der Fahrkartenschalter ?

voh ist dair far'-kart-en-shult'-er

First (second) class return to Hamburg	Hamburg hin und zurück, erster (zweiter) Klasse

hum'-boorg hin ŏŏnt tsŏŏ-rück' airst'-er (tsvī'-ter) kluss'er

Two singles to Cologne	Köln zweimal

kurln tsvī'-mahl

Single ticket	Einfache Fahrkarte

ine'-faCH-er far'-kart-er

Please write down the price	Bitte, schreiben Sie den Preis auf

bitt'-er shrī'-ben zee dane price owf

Where can I get a platform ticket ?	Wo bekommt man Bahnsteig-karten ?

voh bek-ommt' mun bahn'-shtīg-kart-en

Which is the way to the trains ?	Wie komme ich zu den Zügen ?

vee komm'-er ich tsoo dane tsü'-gen

Which platform does the train go from ?	Von welchem Bahnsteig fährt der Zug ab?

fon vellch'em bahn'-shtīg fairt der tsoog up

Is it an express ?	Ist es ein Schnellzug?

ist ez ine shnell'-tsoog

Is there a supplementary charge ?	Muss ich Zuschlag zahlen?

mōōss ich tsoo'-shlahg tsah'-len

When does the train for . . . go ?	Wann fährt der Zug nach . . . ab?

vunn fairt dair tsoog naCH . . . up

Is there a dining-car (sleeping-car) on the train ?	Hat der Zug Speisewagen (Schlafwagen)?

hut dair tsoog shpī'-zer vah-gen (shlahf'-vah-gen)

How much extra does it cost !	Was kostet es extra?

vuss kost'-et ez extra

Must I (can I) reserve a seat ?	Muss ich (kann ich) einen Platz belegen?

mōōss ich (kunn ich) i'-nen pluts ber'-lay'-gen

Are there any seats (berths) left ?	Gibt es noch Plätze (Betten)?

geebt ez noCH plet'-ser (bet'-en)

Is the train in ?	Ist der Zug schon da?

ist dair tsoog shōn dah

Is the train busy ?	Ist der Zug voll?

ist dair tsoog foll

Where is the left-luggage ?	Wo ist der Gepäckschalter?

voh ist dair gep-eck-shull'-ter

Where do I register my luggage?	Wo gebe ich mein Gepäck auf?

voh gay'-ber ich mine gep-eck' owf

Please register these pieces for me	Bitte, geben Sie diese Stücke für mich auf

bitt'-er gay'-ben zee dee'-zer shtük'-er für mich owf

I want to send these bags through to . . .	Ich möchte diese Koffer direkt nach . . . senden

ich murch'-ter dee'-zer koff'-er dee-rect naCH . . . zen'-den

Register my luggage and bring the slip back quickly	Geben Sie mein Gepäck auf und bringen Sie mir schnell den Schein

gay'-ben zee mine gep-eck' owf öönt bring'-en zee mere shnell dane shine

I want to insure my luggage	Ich möchte mein Gepäck ver-sichern

ich murch'-ter mine gep-eck' fair-zich'-ern

How much is there to pay?	Was kostet es?

vuss kost'-et ez

How much do you charge for each?	Was kostet das Stück?

vuss kost'-et duss shtük

Please keep an eye on my things till I find a porter	Bitte, passen Sie auf meine Sachen auf, bis ich einen Träger finde

bitt'-er pus'-en zee owf mi'-ner zaCH'-en owf biss ich i'-nen tray'-ger fin'-der

Porter, take my luggage to the train for . . .	Träger, bringen Sie mein Gepäck zum Zug nach . . .

tray'-ger bring'-en zee mine gep-eck' tsööm tsoog naCH . . .

I should like a corner seat (window seat)	Ich möchte einen Eckplatz, (Fensterplatz) haben

ich murch'-ter i'-nen eck'-pluts (fen'-ster-pluts) haben

Facing (back to) the engine	Vorwärts (Rückwärts)

for'-vairts (rük'-vairts)

Is this seat taken?	Ist dieser Platz frei?

ist dee'-zer pluts fry

This seat is taken	Dieser Platz ist besetzt

dee'-zer pluts ist bez-etst'

I have reserved a seat	Ich habe einen Platz reserviert

ich hah'-ber i'-nen pluts ray'-ser'-veert

Put my luggage on the rack please	Bitte, legen Sie mein Gepäck ins Netz

bitt'-er lay'-gen zee mine gep'-eck inz nets

Excuse me please	Entschuldigen Sie bitte

ent-shööl-dig-en zee bitt'-er

Perhaps you would let us sit together ?	Würden Sie uns zusammen sitzen lassen?
	vür′-den zee ōōns tsōō-zamm′-en zits′-en luss′-en
Not in the least	Nicht im geringsten
	nicht im ger-ing′-sten
It's quite all right	Bitte schön
	bitt′-er schurn
Do you mind if I smoke ?	Stört es Sie wenn ich rauche?
	shturt ez zee, venn ich rowCH-er
Can you give me a light, please ?	Können Sie mir bitte Feuer geben
	kurn′-en zee mere bitt′-er foy′-er gay′-ben
May I open the window ?	Darf ich das Fenster aufmachen?
	darf ich duss fen′-ster owf′-maCH′-en
Would you shut the window ?	Würden Sie das Fenster zumachen?
	vür′-den zee duss fen′-ster tsoo′-maCH′-en
Somebody is sitting in my place	Jemand sitzt auf meinem Platz
	yay′-munt zitst owf mī′-nem pluts
Here is my ticket	Hier ist meine Fahrkarte
	here ist mī′-ner far′-kar-ter
What station is this ?	Wie heisst dieser Bahnhof?
	vee hisst dee′-zer bahn′-höf
How long does the train stop ?	Wie lange hält der Zug?
	vee lung′-er helt dair tsoog
Can I get out ?	Kann ich aussteigen?
	kun ich owce′-shtī-gen
Have I time to go to the refreshment room ?	Habe ich Zeit in den Speisesaal zu gehen?
	hah′-ber ich tsite, in dane shpī′-zer-zahl tsoo gay′-en
Where is the refreshment room ?	Wo ist der Speisesaal?
	vo ist dair shpī′-zer-zahl
Tickets please	Fahrkarten bitte
	far′-kart-en bitt′-er

Where is the guard (attendant)? Wo ist der Zugführer
(Schaffner)?

vo ist dair tsoog'-für-er, (shuff'-ner)

Must I change trains? Muss ich umsteigen?

mōoss ich ōōm'-shtī-gen

Where must I change? Wo muss ich umsteigen?

voh mōoss ich ōōm'-shtī'-gen

Where does the other train go from? Wo fährt der andere Zug ab?

voh fairt dair un'-der-er tsoog up

Is there an immediate con-nection? Habe ich direkten Anschluss?

hah'-ber ich dee-rect'-en un'-schlōōss

Is it a through train to . . .? Fährt der Zug nach . . . durch?

fairt dair tsoog naCH . . . dōōrch

How long have I to wait? Wie lange muss ich warten?

vee lung'-er mōōss ich vart'-en

Does this train go to . . .? Fährt dieser Zug nach . . . ?

fairt dee-zer tsoog naCH . . .

Does this train pass through . . .? Fährt dieser Zug über . . . ?

fairt dee-zer tsoog ü'-ber . . .

Does the train stop at . . .? Hält der Zug in . . .?

helt dair tsoog in . . .

Are we nearly there? Sind wir bald da?

zint vere bult dah

How much longer is it? Wie lange dauert es noch?

vee lung'-er dow'-ert ez noCH

We are very late Wir haben viel Verspätung

vere hah'-ben feel fair-shpate'-ōōng

We are on time Wir haben keine Verspätung

vere hah'-ben kī'-ner fairshpate'-ōōng

Where are we now? Wo sind wir jetzt?

voh zint vere yetst

Is that near . . .? Ist das in der Nähe von . . .?

ist duss in dair nay'-er fon . . .

Can I get . . . on the train ?   Kann ich . . . im Zug bekommen?

kun ich . . . im tsoog bek-omm'-en

Can I have an upper (lower) berth ?   Kann ich ein oberes (unteres) Bett haben?

kunn ich ine ō'-ber-ez (ōōnt'-er-ez) bett' hah'-ben

I want a pillow (rug)   Ich möchte ein Kissen (eine Decke)

ich murcht'-er ine kiss'-en (i'-ner deck'-er)

What time is breakfast (lunch, tea, dinner) ?   Wann gibt es Frühstück (Mittagessen, Tee, Abendessen)?

vun geebt ez frü'-shtük (mitt'-ahg-ess-en, tay, ah'-bent-ess-en)

When do we arrive ?   Wann kommen wir an?

vun komm'-en vere un

Wake me at . . .   Wecken Sie mich um . . .

veck'-en zee mich ōōm . . .

Bring me a cup of tea (coffee) in the morning   Bringen Sie mir eine Tasse Tee (Kaffee) am Morgen

bring'-en zee mere i'-ner tuss'-er tay (kuff'-ay) um morg'-en

Porter, take my luggage and find me a taxi   Träger, nehmen Sie mein Gepäck und besorgen Sie mir ein Taxi.

tray'-ger nay'-men zee mine gep-eck' oont be-zor'-gen zee mere ine tux'-ee

I have missed my train   Ich habe meinen Zug verpasst

ich hah'-ber mī-nen tsoog fair-pust

Is there another train this evening ?   Fährt heute abend ein anderer Zug?

fairt hoyt'-er ah'-bent ine under'-er tsoog

I have got into the wrong train   Ich habe den falschen Zug genommen

ich hah'-ber dane ful-shen tsoog gay-nomm-en

Is there a hotel nearby ?   Ist ein Hotel in der Nähe?

ist ine ho'-tell in dair nay'-er

PLANE

VOCABULARY

air hostess, die Flugbegleiterin (floog-ber-glite-er-in)
airline, die Fluggesellschaft (floog-ger-zel'-shaft)
airport, der Flughafen (floog'-haf-en)
air-sickness, die Luftkrankheit (looft'-krunk-hite)
cloud, die Wolke (volk'-er)
crew, die Besatzung (ber-zats'-oong)
cotton-wool, die Watte (vutt'-er)
fog, der Nebel (nay-bel)
jet aircraft, das Düsenflugzeug (düs'-en-floog'-tsoyg)
land, to, landen (lun'-den)
passenger, der Passagier (pass-ah-jeer)
pilot, der Pilote (pi'-loht'-er)
plane, das Flugzeug (floog'-tsoyg)
propellor, der Propeller (pro'-pell'-er)
runway, die Rollbahn (roll'-bahn)
seat, der Platz (pluts)
seat back, die Lehne (lane'-er)
seat belt, der Gurt (Sicherheits-) (goort) (zich-air-hites)
steward, der Steward (stay'-vart)
take off, der Abflug (up-floog)
tray, das Tablett (tah-blet')
window, das Fenster (fen'-ster)
wing, der Flügel (flü'-gel)

How do I get to the Airline Office ?	**Wie komme ich zum Büro der Fluggesellschaft?**

vee komm'-er ich tsoom bü-ro' dair floog-ger-zel'-shaft

Is there a plane from here to . . . ?	**Fliegt ein Flugzeug von hier nach. . .?**

fleecht ine floog'-tsoyg fon here naCH . . .

When does the plane leave ?	**Wann fliegt das Flugzeug ab?**

vun fleecht duss floog'-tsoyg up

When do we land in . . . ?	**Wann landen wir in . . .?**

vun lund'-en vere in . . .

What is the fare (return) ?	**Was kostet es (hin und zurück)?**

vuss kost'-et ez (hin oont tsoo-rük')

I want to reserve a seat in the plane leaving tomorrow morning for . . .	Ich möchte einen Platz in dem Flugzeug belegen, das morgen früh nach . . . fliegt

ich murch'-ter i'-nen pluts in dame floog'-tsoyg bel-ay'-gen, duss mor'-gen frü naCH . . . fleecht

How do I get to the airport ?	Wie komme ich zum Flughafen?

vee komm'-er ich tsŏŏm floog'-haf-en

A motor-coach leaves from outside this office at . . .	Ein Autobus fährt von der Tür dieses Büros um . . . ab

ine ow'-to-bŏŏss fairt fon dair tür dee'-zez bü-rŏz ŏŏm . . . up

How much luggage may I take without paying extra ?	Wieviel Gepäck darf ich mitnehmen ohne extra zu bezahlen?

vee-feel' gep-eck darf ich mit'-nay-men ō'-ner extra tsoo bay-tsahl'-en

What do you charge for the luggage ?	Was kostet das Gepäck?

vuss kost'-et duss gep-eck

There is fog at Düsseldorf	Nebel in Düsseldorf

nay'-bel in düss'-el-dōrf

Do we land anywhere before we reach . . . ?	Landen wir irgendwo, bevor wir nach . . . kommen?

lund'-en vere ear'-gent-voh, bef-ōr' vere naCH . . . komm'-en

Can I change my seat ?	Kann ich meinen Platz wechseln?

kun ich mī'-nen pluts vex'-eln

I cannot fasten my seatbelt	Ich kann meinen Gurt nicht zumachen

ich kun mī'-nen gŏŏrt nicht tsoo-maCH'-en

I should like a cup of tea (coffee)	Ich hätte gern eine Tasse Tee (Kaffee)

ich hett'-er gairn i'-ner tuss'-er tay (kuff'-ay)

I feel sick	Mir ist schlecht

mere ist shlecht

Bring me a brandy, please	Bringen Sie mir einen Cognac bitte

bring'-en zee mere i'-nen konn'-yak bitt'-er

Is the luggage examined at the airport ?	Wird das Gepäck am Flughafen kontrolliert?

virt duss gep-eck' um floog'-hah-fen kon-trol-eert'

COACH, BUS, UNDERGROUND, TAXI

VOCABULARY

bus, der Autobus (ow'-to-booss)
change, to, umsteigen (oom'-shti-gen)
conductor, der Schaffner (shuff'-ner)
connection, der Anschluss (un-shlooss)
fare, das Fahrgeld (far'-gelt)
stop, die Haltestelle (hult'-er-shtell-er)
taxi, das Taxi (tux'-ee)
terminus, die Endhaltestelle (ent'-hult-er-shtell-er)
ticket, der Fahrschein (far'-shine)
tram, die Strassenbahn (shtrahss'-en-bahn)
tube station, der Untergrundbahnhof (oon'-ter-groont-bahn-höf)
underground, die Untergrundbahn (oon'-tergroont-bahn)

Would you be so good as to direct me to . . .	Würden Sie so gut sein, mir den Weg nach . . . zu zeigen?

vürd'-en zee zo goot zine, mere dane vaig naCH . . . tsoo tsi'-gen

Can I walk or must I take a taxi ?	Kann ich zu Fuss gehen, oder muss ich ein Taxi nehmen?

kun ich tsoo fooss gay'-en, o'-der mooss ich ine tux'-ee nay'-men

Can I go by bus (tram, underground) ?	Kann ich mit dem Autobus (der Strassenbahn, der Untergrundbahn) fahren?

kun ich mit dame ow'-to-booss (dair shtrahss'-en-bahn, dair oon'-ter-groont-bahn) far'-en

Where is the nearest bus stop (tram stop) ?	Wo ist die nächste Haltestelle?

voh ist dee next'-er hult'-er-shtell-er

Where is the tube station ?	Wo ist der Untergrundbahn-hof?
	voh ist dair ŏŏn'-ter-grŏŏnt-bahn-hŏf
Which bus (tram) do I have to take ?	Welchen Bus (welche Strassen-bahn) muss ich nehmen?
	vellch'-en bŏŏss (vellch'-er shtrahss'-en-bahn) mŏŏss ich nay'-men
Does this tram go to . . . ?	Fährt diese Bahn zum . . .?
	fairt dee'-zer bahn tsŏŏm . . .
Where do I have to get off ?	Wo muss ich aussteigen?
	voh mŏŏss ich ows-shtī-gen
I want to get off at . . .	Ich möchte am . . . aussteigen
	ich murch'-ter um . . . ows-shtī-gen
At the next stop	An der nächsten Haltestelle
	un dair next'-en hult'-er-shtell-er
Do I have to change ?	Muss ich umsteigen?
	mŏŏss ich ŏŏm'-shtī'-gen
Can I take this suitcase with me?	Kann ich diesen Koffer mit-nehmen?
	kun ich dee-zen koff'-er mit'-nay-men
Is that the terminus ?	Ist das die Endhaltestelle?
	ist duss dee ent'-hult-er-shtell-er
Call me a taxi	Holen Sie mir ein Taxi
	hole-en zee mere ī'ne tux'-ee
Please drive to . . .	Bitte fahren Sie nach . . .
	bitt'-er far'-en zee naCH . . .
Go quickly I am in a hurry	Fahren Sie schnell Ich habe es eilig
	far'-en zee shnell ich hah'-ber ez ī'-lich

HOTELS

If difficulties arise in obtaining accommodation, the local *Verkehrsamt* will be able to assist.

In country districts the *Gasthof* offers a limited number of reasonably priced rooms.

Breakfast consists of coffee and rolls and is not normally included in the price of the room. A more substantial meal may be had if the traveller requires it.

In health resorts a municipal tax (*Kurtaxe*) is often added to the bill. Inquire about this point when booking rooms.

Sample letter booking a room in advance

A letter booking a room in one of the larger hotels may be written in English, but it is advisable to write in German, if possible, to avoid misunderstanding. A sample letter with translation is given below and it can be easily adapted to meet different requirements. It is also advisable to enclose an International Reply Coupon for a prompt reply. This can be bought from any Post Office.

Dear Sir (Madam),
I wish to reserve one/two, etc. single/double room(s) (with bath) for ... nights from the ... (date).
I shall be glad if you will let me know your price for sleeping accommodation only/half board/full board. I enclose an International Reply Coupon.

Yours faithfully,

Sehr geehrter Herr (geehrte Frau),
Ich möchte ein/zwei Einzelzimmer/Doppelzimmer (mit Bad) für ... Nächte vom ... bis zum ... reservieren.
Ich wäre Ihnen sehr verbunden, könnten Sie mir Ihre Preise für Übernachtung allein/mit Frühstück und Mittagessen/volle Pension mitteilen.
Ich lege einen Internationalen Antwortschein bei.

Hochachtungsvoll,

VOCABULARY

armchair, der Sessel (zess'-el)
bath, das Bad (baht)
bathroom, das Badezimmer (bahd'-er-tsimm-er)
bed, das Bett (bett')
bedroom, das Schlafzimmer (shlahf-tsimm'-er)
bedroom (single), das Einzelzimmer (ine'-tsel-tsimm'-er)
bedroom (double), das Doppelzimmer (dopp'-el-tsimm'-er)
bell, die Klingel (kling'-el)
bill, die Rechnung (rech'-nŏong)
boarding-house, die Pension (pŏn-tsee-on')
board (full), volle Pension (foll'-er pŏn-tsee-on')
blanket, die Decke (deck'-er)
bulb (electric light), die Birne (beer'-ner)
chair, der Stuhl (shtool)
chambermaid, das Zimmermädchen (tsimm-er-maid-chen)
child, das Kind (kint)
coathanger, der Bügel (bü'-gel)
cook, der Koch (koCH)
cot, das Kinderbett (kint'-er-bett')

curtain, die Gardine (gahr-dee'-ner)
dining-room, der Speisesaal (shpī'-zer-zahl)
eiderdown, die Steppdecke (shtep-deck'-er)
floor (storey), das Stockwerk (shtock-vairk)
hotel, das Hotel (ho-tell')
hot-water bottle, die Wärmflasche (verm-flush'-er)
inn, der Gasthof (gust-hōf)
key, der Schlüssel (shlüss'-el)
landing, der Treppenabsatz (trepp'-en-up-zuts)
lavatory, die Toilette (twa-lett'-er)
lift, der Fahrstuhl (far'-shtool)
lounge, die Halle (hull'-er)
manager, der Direktor (dee-rect'-or)
mattress, die Matratze (mut'-ruts'-er)
night porter, der Nachtportier (naCHt'-port-yay)
number, die Nummer (nŏŏm'-er)
office, das Büro (bü-ro)
poster, das Plakat (plah'-kaht)
press, to, bügeln (büg'-eln)
pillow, das Kopfkissen (kopf'-kiss-en)
plug (electric), die Steckdose (shteck'-do'-zer)
proprietor, der Inhaber (in-hah'-ber)
radiator, der Heizkörper (hīts'-kurp'-er)
reading-lamp, die Leselampe (lay-zer-lump'-er)
room (single), das Einzelzimmer (ine'-tsel-tsimm'-er)
room (double), das Doppelzimmer (dopp'-el-tsimm'-er)
receipt, die Quittung (k-vitt'-oong)
sitting-room, das Wohnzimmer (vone'-tsimm'-er)
sheet, das Laken (lah'-ken)
shower, die Dusche (doosh'-er)
shutter, der Fensterladen (fen'-ster-lah-den)
staircase, die Treppe (trepp'-er)
switch, der Schalter (shul'-ter)
table, der Tisch (tish)
tap, der Wasserhahn (vuss'-er-hahn)
terrace, die Terrasse (tair'-uss'-er)
towel, das Handtuch (hunt'-tŏŏCH)
wardrobe, der Schrank (shrunk)
water (warm, cold), das Wasser (warm, kalt) (vuss'-er, varm, kult)
washbasin, das Waschbecken (vush-beck'-en)
window, das Fenster (fen'-ster)

Can you recommend a small hotel?   Können Sie ein kleines Hotel empfehlen?

kurn'-en zee ine kline-ez ho-tell' emp-fay-len

Which is the best hotel?   Welches ist das beste Hotel?

velch'-ez ist duss best'-er ho-tell'

Have you any rooms vacant ? Haben Sie Zimmer frei?
hah'-ben zee tsimm'-er fry

Can you recommend another hotel ? Können Sie mir ein anderes Hotel empfehlen?
kurn'-en zee mere ine un'-der-ez ho-tell' emp-fail'-en

I want a quiet room Ich möchte ein ruhiges Zimmer
ich murcht'-er ine roo-ig'-es tsimm'-er

Have you a room looking on to the river (garden, mountains)? Haben Sie ein Zimmer, von dem man den Fluss (den Garten, die Berge) sehen kann?
hah'-ben zee ine tsimm'-er, fon dame mun dane flooss (dane gahr'-ten, dee bairg'-er) zay-en kun

I want a single room (double room) Ich möchte ein Einzelzimmer (Doppelzimmer)
ich murch'-ter ine ine'-tsel-tsimm'-er (dopp'-el-tsimm'-er)

I want a room with two beds Ich möchte ein Zimmer mit zwei Betten
ich murch'-ter ine tsimm'-er mit tsvi bett'-en

Can we have a cot in our room ? Können wir ein Kinderbett in unserem Zimmer haben?
kurn'-en vere ine kint'-er-bett' in ōōn'-zer-em tsimm'-er hah'-ben

And a bath Und Bad
ōōnt baht

For one night only Nur für eine Nacht
noor für i'-ner naCHt

For a week, perhaps longer Für eine Woche, vielleicht länger
für i'-ner voCH'-er, feel-icht' leng'-er

What is the price of this room (these rooms) ? Was kostet dieses Zimmer (Was kosten diese Zimmer)?
vuss kost'-et dee'-zez tsimm'-er (vuss kost'-en dee'-zer tsimm'-er)

That is too expensive Das ist zu teuer
duss ist tsōū'-er

Have you anything cheaper ?	Haben Sie etwas Billigeres ?
	hah'-ben zee et'-vuss bill'-ig-er-ez
What are the terms with full board ?	Was kostet es mit voller Pension?
	vuss kost'-et ez mit foll'-er pōñ-tsee-on'
How much do you charge for the child (children) ?	Wieviel verlangen Sie für das Kind (die Kinder)
	vee-feel fair-lung-en zee fur duss kint' (dee kint'-er)
How much is bed and breakfast ?	Was kostet das Zimmer mit Frühstück?
	vuss kost'-et duss tsimm'-er mit frü'-shtük
Have you a restaurant ?	Haben Sie ein Restaurant ?
	hah'-ben zee ine rest'-or-ōñ
I will take this room	Ich nehme dieses Zimmer
	ich nay'-mer dee'-zez tsimm'-er
Have our luggage sent up	Lassen Sie unser Gepäck heraufbringen
	luss'-en zee ōōn'-zer gep-eck' hair-owf'-bring-en
Have my luggage fetched from the station	Lassen Sie mein Gepäck vom Bahnhof abholen
	luss'-en zee mine gep-eck' fom bahn'-hof up-hole'-en
Where is the bathroom (W.C.)?	Wo ist das Badezimmer (die Toilette)?
	vo ist duss bahd'-er-tsimm'-er (dee twa-lett-er)
I am going to bed at once	Ich gehe sofort zu Bett
	ich gay'-er zoh-fort tsoo bett'
I am expecting a gentleman (a young lady)	Ich erwarte einen Herrn (eine junge Dame)
	ich air-vart'-er i'-nen hairn (i'-ner yōōng'-er dah'-mer)
Please send him (her) up at once	Bitte schicken Sie ihn (sie) sofort herauf
	bitt'-er shick'-en zee een (zee) zo'-fort hair'-owf
I shall be back at three	Ich werde um drei Uhr zurück sein.
	ich vaird'-er ōōm dry oor tsoo-rük' zine

Is the room ready yet ?	Ist das Zimmer schon fertig ?
	ist duss tsimm'-er shone fair'-tich
I should like another pillow (another blanket)	Ich möchte noch ein Kopfkissen (eine Decke) haben
	ich murch'-ter noCH ine kopf'-kiss-en (ī'-ner deck'-er) hah'-ben
Will you bring me some hot water (soap, towels) ?	Bringen Sie mir bitte heisses Wasser (Seife, Handtücher) ?
	bring'-en zee mere bitt'-er hice'-ez vuss'-er (zī'-fer, hunt'-tüch-er)
I should like some drinking-water please	Bringen Sie bitte etwas Trinkwasser
	bring'-en-zee bitt'-er et'-vuss trink-vuss'-er
I want to have a hot bath	Ich möchte ein heisses Bad
	ich murch'-ter ine hice'-ez baht
The sheets on this bed are damp	Die Laken im Bett sind feucht
	dee lah'-ken im bett zint foycht
This room is not clean	Dieses Zimmer ist nicht sauber
	dee'-zez tsimm'-er ist nicht zow'-ber
The bulb is broken	Die Birne ist kaputt
	dee beer'-ner ist kah'-poot
Is there a plug for my electric razor?	Ist ein Stecker für meinen elektrischen Rasierapparat da ?
	ist ine shtek'-er für mī'-nen ay-lek'-trish-en rah'-zeer-a-par-aht dah
Can you wash some things for me by tomorrow?	Können Sie einige Sachen für mich bis morgen waschen ?
	kurn'-en zee ī'-nig-er saCH'-en für mich bis morg'-en vush'-en
There is a button missing	Es fehlt ein Knopf
	ez failt ine knopf
This zip-fastener is broken	Dieser Reissverschluss ist entzwei
	dee'-zer rice'-fair-shlõoss ist ent'-tsvī
I have two pairs of socks to be mended	Ich habe zwei Paar Socken zum stopfen
	ich hah'-ber tsvī pahr zock'-en tsõom shtopf'-en

Please have these clothes dried   Bitte lassen Sie diese Sachen trocknen

bitt'-er luss'-en zee dee'-zer saCH'-en tröck'-nen

These shoes are not mine   Diese Schuhe gehören mir nicht

dee'-zer shoo'-er ger'-hur-en mere nicht

Have you any English newspapers?   Haben Sie englische Zeitungen?

hah'-ben zee eng'-lish-er tsite'-ōōng-en

What does it cost to send a letter to . . .?   Was kostet ein Brief nach . . .?

vuss kost'-et ine brief naCH . . .?

I want to send a telegram   Ich möchte ein Telegramm aufgeben

ich murcht'-er ine tel-ay-grumm' owf'-gay-ben

I want to telephone   Ich möchte telephonieren

ich murcht'-er tel-er-phone-eer'-en

Where can I buy . . .   Wo kann ich . . . kaufen?

voh kun ich . . . kowf'-en

Bring me some writing materials (some paper, some envelopes)   Bringen Sie mir bitte Schreibmaterial (etwas Papier, einige Briefumschläge)

bring'-en zee mere bitt'er shribe'-ma-ter'-ree-ahl (et'-vuss pup-eer, i'-nig-er brief-ōōm'-shlay-ger)

Have you a time-table of the trains for . . .?   Haben Sie einen Fahrplan für die Züge nach . . .?

hah'-ben zee i'-nen far'-plahn für dee tsü'-ger nach . . .

There is a draught   Es zieht

ez tseet

Can we have an English breakfast?   Können wir englisches Frühstück haben?

kurn'-en vere eng'-lish-ez frü'-shtük hah'-ben

Can I have breakfast in my room?   Kann ich in meinem Zimmer frühstücken?

kun ich in mi'-nem tsimm'-er frü'-shtük'-en

We shall not be here for lunch (dinner) today (tomorrow) — Wir werden zum Mittagessen (Abendessen) nicht hier sein heute (morgen)

vere vaird'-en tsoom mit'-ahg-ess-en (ah'-bent-ess-en) nicht here sine hoy'-ter (morg'-en)

I wish to dine a little earlier (later) — Ich möchte etwas früher (später) essen

ich murcht'-er et'-vuss frü'-er (shpate'-er) ess'-en

We shall be four for dinner this evening — Heute abend werden wir vier Personen zum Essen sein

hoy'-ter ah'-bent vair'-den vere feer pair-zö'-nen tsöōm ess'-en sine

Please call me at ... — Bitte wecken Sie mich um ...

bitt'-er veck'-en zee mich ŏŏm ...

Don't disturb me in the morning — Stören Sie mich nicht morgen früh

shtur'-ren zee mich nicht morg'-en frü

Good night — Gute Nacht

goot'-er naCHt

Who is there? — Wer ist da?

vair ist dah

What time is it? — Wie spät ist es?

vee shpate ist ez

Wait a minute — Einen Moment bitte

i'-nen mö'-ment bitt'-er

Come in! — Herein!

hair-ine'

Have my shoes cleaned — Lassen Sie meine Schuhe putzen

luss'-en zee mī'-ner shoo'-er pŏŏt'-sen

I want my clothes brushed (pressed) — Ich möchte meine Sachen gebürstet (gebügelt) haben

ich murcht'-er mī-ner saCH'-en geb-ürst'-et (geb-ü'-gelt) hah'-ben

Get my shoes (suit) — Bitte, bringen Sie mir meine Schuhe (meinen Anzug)

hitt'-er bring'-en zee mere mī'-ner shoo'-er (mī'-nen un'-tsoog)

Are there any letters for me ?   Sind Briefe für mich ange-
kommen?

zint brief'-er für mich un'-gek-omm-en

Has anyone asked for me ?   Hat jemand nach mir gefragt?

hut yay'-munt naCH mere gef-rahgt

Did anyone ring up for me ?   Hat mich jemand angerufen?

hut mich yay'-munt un'-ger-oof-en

I want to post a letter   Ich möchte einen Brief aufgeben

ich murcht'-er i'-nen brief owf'-gay-ben

Is . . . still in his (her) room ?   Ist . . . noch in seinem
(ihrem) Zimmer?

ist . . . noCH in zi'-nem (ee'-rem) tsimm'-er

**What is the number of . . .
room ?**   Welche Nummer hat . . .
Zimmer?

velch'-er nōōm'-er hut . . . tsimm'-er

Will you send up a messenger ?   Bitte schicken Sie einen Boten
hinauf?

bitt'-er shick'-en zee i'-nen boat'-en hin-owf'

Is there a night porter on duty ?   Ist ein Nachtportier hier?

ist ine naCHt'-port-yay here

**Shall I be able to get anything
to eat on my return ?**   Kann ich etwas zu essen
bekommen, wenn ich
zurückkomme?

kunn ich et'-vuss tsoo ess'-en bek-omm'-en, venn ich tsoo-rük'-komm'-er

**The chambermaid never comes
when I ring**   Das Zimmermädchen kommt
nie wenn ich klingle

duss tsimm'-er-mate'-shen kommt' nee ven ich kling'-ler

I have lost . . . in my room   Ich habe . . . in meinem Zimmer
verloren

ich hah'-ber . . . in mi'-nem tsimm'-er fair-lō'-ren

**I have just had a letter (tele-
gram)**   Ich habe gerade einen Brief
(ein Telegramm) bekommen

ich hah'-ber ger-rah'-der i'-nen brief (ine tel-ay-grumm') ber'-komm-en

I must leave at once   Ich muss sofort abreisen

ich mōōss zo-fort up'-ri-zen

I am taking the . . . train	Ich nehme den Zug nach . . .

ich nay'-mer dane tsoog naCH . . .

I want to see the Manager	Ich möchte den Direktor sprechen

ich murcht'-er dane dee-rect'-or shprech-en

Get my bill ready, please	Bitte machen Sie meine Rechnung fertig

bitt'-er maCH'-en zee mi'-ner rech'-nŏŏng fair'-tich

Will you take a traveller's cheque ?	Nehmen Sie einen Reise-scheck ?

nay'-men zee i'-nen ri'-zer-sheck

How much does the bill come to?	Wieviel macht die Rechnung?

vee-feel' maCHt dee rech'-nŏŏng

What are these charges for ?	Wofür sind diese Beträge?

vo-für zint dee'-zer bur ray'-ger

I think you have made a mistake	Ich glaube, Sie haben sich geirrt

ich glow'-ber zee hah'-ben sich ge-irrt'

We did not have . . .	Wir haben kein . . . gehabt

vere hah'-ben kine . . . ge-hupt'

You said the rooms only cost ...	Sie sagten, die Zimmer kosten nur ...

zee zaCHt'-en, dee tsimm'-er kost'-en noor ...

Please give me a receipt	Bitte geben Sie mir eine Quittung

bitt'-er gay'-ben zee mere i'-ner k-vitt'-ŏŏng

Is the service charge added ?	Ist die Bedienung einbegriffen?

ist dee bed-een'-ŏŏng ine-beg'-riff'-en

Divide that between you	Teilen Sie das unter sich

tile'-en zee duss ŏŏn'-ter zeech

I am leaving tonight	Ich reise heute abend ab

ich ri'-zer hoy'-ter ah'-bent up

Have my luggage brought down	Lassen Sie mein Gepäck herunterbringen

luss'-en zee mine gep'-eck hair-ŏŏn'-ter-bring-en

Send my luggage to the station   Schicken Sie mein Gepäck zum Bahnhof

shick'-en zee mine gep-eck' tsōōm bahn'-hōf

Get me a taxi, please   Bitte, bestellen Sie mir ein Taxi

bitt'-er ber-shtell'-en zee mere i'ne tux'-ee

How long does it take to the station ?   Wie lange brauche ich zum Bahnhof?

vee lung'-er browCH'-er ich tsōōm bahn'-hōf

I have been very comfortable   Ich habe mich sehr wohl gefühlt

ich hah'-ber mich zair vole gef-ült'

If any letters come for me, please forward them to . . .   Sollten noch Briefe für mich ankommen, senden Sie sie bitte an . . .

zolt'-en noCH brief'-er für mich un'-komm-en, zend'-en zee zee bitt'-er un . . .

Have some sandwiches packed for me to take on the journey   Lassen Sie bitte ein paar belegte Brote für die Reise einpacken.

luss'-en zee bitt'-er ine par bel-aygt'-er brō'-ter für dee rī'-zer ine'-puck-en

Here is my key   Hier ist mein Schlüssel

here ist mine shlüss'-el

Thank you and good-bye   Danke sehr und auf Wiedersehen

dunk'-er zair oont owf vee'-der-zay-en

N.B.—For further details of meals in hotels see under RESTAURANTS, *page 36.*

LAUNDRY AND CLEANING

For vocabulary see under SHOPPING: CLOTHES, *page 103.*

I have some things for the laundry   Ich möchte etwas gewaschen haben

ich murch'-ter et'-vuss ger'-vush'-en hah'-ben

When are the things returned ?	Wann kann ich die Sachen zurückbekommen?

vunn kunn ich dee saCH'-en tsoo-rück-ber'-komm-en

Let me have the shirts and collars back as soon as possible, I am not in such a hurry for the rest	Die Hemden und Kragen brauche ich so bald wie möglich, das Übrige eilt nicht so sehr

dee hemt'-en ōōnt krah'-gen browCH'-er ich zo bult vee murg'-lich, duss ü'-brig-er īlt nicht zo zair

Can I have these things back in two days ?	Kann ich diese Sachen in zwei Tage wieder haben?

kunn ich dee'-zer saCH'-en in tsvī tahg'-er vee'-der hah'-ben

Can you get my suit cleaned ?	Können Sie bitte meinen Anzug reinigen lassen?

kurn'-en zee bitt'-er mī'-nen un'-tsoog rine'-i-gen luss'-en

Some of the things want mending	Einige Sachen müssen gestopft werden

ī'-nig'-er saCH'-en müss'-en gesh-topft' vair'-den

Can you sew on this button for me?	Können Sie den Knopf für mich annähen?

kurn'-en zee dane knopf für mich un'-nay'-en

SIGHTSEEING

VOCABULARY

battlement, die Zinne (tsinn'-er)
building, das Gebäude (geb-oy'-der)
bridge, die Brücke (brük'er)
cable car, die Seilbahn (zile'-bahn)
castle, das Schloss (shloss)
cathedral, der Dom (dome)
church, die Kirche (keerch'-er)
excursion, der Ausflug (owce'-floog)
gardens (botanical), der botanische Garten (bot-ahn'-ish-er gart'-en)
gardens (zoological), der zoologische Garten (tso-lo'-gish-er gart'-en)
guide, der Führer (für'-er)
interpreter, der Dolmetscher (dol'-metch-er)
lake, der See (zay)
law courts, die Gerichte (ger'-ich-ter)

memorial, das Denkmal (denk′-mahl)
mountain, der Berg (bairg)
museum, das Museum (moo-zay′-ōōm)
picture gallery, die Gemälde Galerie (ge-meld′-er gal-er-ee)
river, der Fluss (flooss)
souvenir, das Andenken (un-denk-en)
square, der Platz (pluts)
steamer, der Dampfer (dump′-fer)
street, die Strasse (strahss′-er)
town hall, das Rathaus (raht′-house)

Where can I get a guide-book in English (a map of the town) ?	Wo kann ich ein Reisehandbuch in englisch (einen Stadtplan) bekommen?

voh kun ich ine ri′-zer-hunt-booCH in eng′-lish (ī′-nen shtutt-plahn) ber-komm′-en

I want an English-speaking guide	Ich möchte einen Führer, der englisch spricht

ich murcht′-er i′-nen für′-er dare eng′-lish shpricht

How much ought I to give the guide ?	Wieviel muss ich dem Führer geben?

vee-feel mōōs ich dame für′-er gay′-ben

We don't need a guide	Wir brauchen keinen Führer

vere browCH-en ki′-nen für′-er

I was looking for . . . and I took the wrong road	Ich habe . . . gesucht und habe die falsche Strasse genommen

ich hah′-ber . . . ger′-zooCHt ōōnt hah′-ber dee falsh′-er shtrahss′-er ger′-nomm-en

Is this the right way to . . .?	Komme ich auf diesem Wege nach . . .?

komm′-er ich owf dee′-zem vorig′-er naCH . . .

Would you be so good as to direct me to . . . ?	Würden Sie so gut sein, mir den Weg nach . . . zu zeigen?

vürd′-en zee zo goot zine, mere dane vaig naCH . . . tsoo tsi′-gen

Straight ahead	Gerade aus

ger-rah′-der owce

First on the right	Die Erste rechts

dee airst′-er rechts

Second on the left	Die Zweite links
	dee tsvī'-ter links
Keep straight on	Immer gerade aus
	imm'-er ger-rah'-der owce
What street (church, building) is that ?	Was ist das für eine Strasse (Kirche, ein Gebäude)?
	vuss ist duss für ī'-ner strahss'-er, keerch'-er, ine geb-oy'-der
Can you direct me to the castle (museum) ?	Können Sie mir bitte den Weg zum Schloss (Museum) zeigen?
	kurn'-en zee mere bitt'-er dane vaig tsoom shloss (moo-zay'-ōōm) tsī'-gen
Can one see over the castle ?	Kann man das Schloss besichtigen?
	kun mun duss shloss bez-icht'-ig-en
How long does . . . stay open ?	Wie lange bleibt . . . offen?
	vee lung'-er blībt . . . off'-en
On what days (when) is . . . open to the public ?	An welchen Tagen (wann) ist . . . für das Publikum geöffnet?
	un vellch'-en tahg'-en (vun) ist . . . für duss poob'-lick-ōōm ge-urf'-net
When does the next tour start ?	Wann beginnt die nächste Führung ?
	vunn beg-innt' dee next'-er für'-ōōng
How long does the tour take ?	Wie lange dauert die Führung?
	vee lung'-er dow'-ert dee für'-ōōng
May I photograph here ?	Darf ich hier photographieren ?
	darf ich here photo-graph-eer'-en
Is that the . . . Memorial ?	Ist das das . . . Denkmal?
	ist duss duss . . . denk'-mahl
Did . . . live in this house ?	Hat . . . in diesem Haus gewohnt?
	hut . . . in dee'-zem house gev-ōnt
How do I get to the old town ?	Wie komme ich zur Altstadt?
	vee komm' er ich tsōōr ult-shtutt

What is the name of that mountain ?	Wie heisst dieser Berg?

vee hisst dee'-zer bairg

Is there a cable car ?	Gibt es eine Seilbahn?

geebt ez i'-ner zile'-bahn

Does one have to walk ?	Muss man zu Fuss gehen?

mŏŏss mun tsoo fooss gay'-en

Is it very far ?	Ist es sehr weit?

ist ez zair vite

Is there a restaurant at the top ?	Gibt es ein Restaurant auf dem Berge?

geebt ez ine rest'-or-ôñ owf dame bairg'-er

Which is the best way back ?	Was ist der beste Weg zurück?

vuss ist dair best'-er vaig tsoo-rük'

SPORT, GAMES AND ENTERTAINMENT

VOCABULARY

SPORT

ball, der Ball (bul)
bowls, das Kegeln (kay'-geln)
cubicle, die Kabine (ka-bee'-ner)
football match, das Fussballspiel (fooss'-bal-shpeel)
goal, das Tor (tore)
Golf, Golf (golf)
    bunker, der Bunker (bŏŏnk'-er)
    caddie, der Caddie (kah'-dee)
    drive, to, treiben (try'-ben)
    golf-club, der Golfschläger (golf'-shlay-ger)
    golf course, der Golfplatz (golf'-pluts)
    green, der Rasen (rah'-zen)
    hole, das Loch (loCH)
    putt, to, einlochen (ine'-loCH-en)
Horse racing, das Pferderennen (pfair'-der-ren-nen)
    bet, die Wette (vet'-er)
    favourite, der Favorit (fah'-vo-reet)
    flat race, das Flachrennen (flaCH-renn'-en)
    (grand) stand, die Tribüne (tree-bü'-ner)
    horse, das Pferd (pfairt)
    jockey, der Jockei (yō'-kī)

race-course, die Rennbahn (renn'-bahn)
steeplechase, das Hindernissrennen (hin'-der-niss-ren-nen)
tote, der Totalisator (to-ta-lee-zah'-tor)
winning-post, das Ziel (tseel)
Ice skating, das Schlittschuhlaufen (shlitt'-shoo'-lowf'-en)
  rink, die Eisbahn (ice'-bahn)
  skate, to, Schlittschuh laufen (shlitt'-shoo lowf'-en)
  skater, der Schlittschuhläufer (shlitt'-shoo-loy'-fer)
  skates, die Schlittschuhe (shlitt'-shoo-er)
miniature golf, das Miniatur Golf (mee-nee-aht'-oor golf)
motor-boat, Motorboot (mo-tōr'-boat)
partner, der Mitspieler (mit'-shpeel'-er)
play, das Spiel (shpeel)
player, der Spieler (shpeel'-er)
relax, to, sich ausruhen (zich owce-roo'-en)
roller-skates, die Rollschuhe (rol'-shoo-er)
score, das Ergebnis (er-gape'-niss)
Ski-ing, das Skilaufen (shee'-lowf'-en)
  skis, die Skier (shee'-er)
  ski-jump, die Sprungschanze (shprŏŏng-shant'-ser)
  ski run, der Skilauf (shee-lowf)
  ski-slopes, das Skigelände (shee'-gel-end er)
  water ski-ing, das Wasserskilaufen (vuss'-er-shee'-lowf'-en)
stadium, das Stadion (shtah'-dee-ōn)
Swimming, das Schwimmen (shvim'-en)
  bathing cap, die Badekappe (bahd'-er-kupp'-er)
  bathing costume, der Badeanzug (bahd'-er-un-tsoog)
  bathing hut, die Badehütte (bahd'-er-hütt'-er)
  boat, das Boot (boat)
  canoe, das Kanu (kah'-noo)
  current, die Strömung (shtrur'-mŏŏng)
  deck-chair, der Liegestuhl (lee'-ger-shtool)
  diving-board, das Sprungbrett (shprŏŏng-brett)
  depth, die Tiefe (teef'-er)
  fish, der Fisch (fish)
  raft, das Floss (flōss)
  swim, to, schwimmen (shvimm'-en)
  swimming-pool, das Schwimmbad (shvim'-baht)
Tennis, Tennis (ten'-iss)
  advantage, der Vorteil (for'-tile)
  deuce, der Ausgleich (owce-glīch)
  doubles, das Doppel (dopp-el)
  game, das Spiel (shpeel)
  love, Null (nŏŏl)
  net, das Netz (nets)
  racket, der Tennisschläger (ten'-iss-shlay-ger
  set, der Satz (zuts)
  service, der Aufschlag, (owf'-shlag)
  singles, das Einzel (ine-tsel)
  tennis court, der Tennisplatz (ten'-iss-pluts)

team, die Mannschaft (mun'-shaft)
tournament, das Turnier (toor-neer')

GAMES

Billiards, Billard (bill'-yard)
    billiard ball, der Billardball (bill'-yard-bul)
    billiard table, der Billardtisch (bill'-yard-tish)
    cue, der Billardstock (bill'-yard-shtŏck)
Bridge, Bridge (as in English)
    ace, das As (uss)
    card (playing), die Spielkarte (shpeel-kart'-er)
    clubs, Treff (treff)
    diamonds, Karo (kah'-ro)
    dummy, der Strohmann (shtro'-mun)
    hearts, Herz (hairts)
    king, der König (kurn'-ich)
    knave, der Bube (boob'-er)
    pack (of cards), das Kartenspiel (kart'-en-shpeel)
    queen, die Königin (kurn'-ig-in)
    spades, Pik (peek)
    stake, der Einsatz (ine'-zuts)
    trick, der Stich (shtich)
    trump (card), die Trumpfkarte (trŏŏmpf-kart'-er)
    trump, to, stechen (shtech'-en)
Chess, Schach (shaCH)
    bishop, der Läufer (loy'-fair)
    castle, der Turm (tŏŏrm)
    chess-board, das Schachbrett (shaCH-brett)
    king, der König (kurn'-ich)
    knight, der Springer (shpring'-er)
    pawn, der Bauer (bow'-er)
    queen, die Königin (kurn'-ig-in)
counter, die Spielmarke (shpeel-mark'-er)
dice, der Würfel (vürf'-el)
dominoes, das Dominospiel (do-mee-no-shpeel)
draughts, das Damenspiel (dah'-men-shpeel)
table-tennis, das Tischtennis (tish-tenn'-is)

ENTERTAINMENT

ball, der Ball (bul)
band, die Kapelle (kup-ell'-er)
box, die Loge (low'-jer)
box-office, die Kasse (kuss'-er)
casino, das Kasino (kass'-ee-no)
cinema, das Kino (keen'-o)
circle, der Rang (rung)
cloakroom, die Garderobe (gahr'-der-row'-ber)
cloakroom ticket, die Garderobenmarke (gahr'-der-row'-ben-mark'-er)

comedy, das Lustspiel (lōōst'-shpeel)
concert, das Konzert (kon-tsairt)
dance-hall, das Tanzlokal (tunts-low-kahl)
dance, to, tanzen (tunts'-en)
dress circle, der erster Rang (airst'-er rung)
entertainment, die Unterhaltung (ōōnt'-er-hull'-tōōng)
fancy-dress ball, der Maskenball (musk'-en-bul)
film, der Film (film)
gallery, die Galerie (gah'-ler-ee)
interval, die Pause (pow'-zer)
night-club, das Nachtlokal (naCHt'-lo-kahl)
newsreel, die Wochenschau (voCH'-en-sh-ow)
opera, die Oper (o'-per)
orchestra, das Orchester (or-kest'-er)
pit, das Parterre (par'-terr)
play, das Schauspiel (show'-shpeel)
programme, das Programm (pro-grumm')
seat, der Platz (pluts)
stage, die Bühne (bü'-ner)
stalls, das Parkett (park-ett')
tango, der Tango (tan-go)
theatre, das Theater (tay-aht'-er)
theatre (open air), die Freilichtbühne (fry-licht-bü'-ner)
upper circle, oberer Rang (o'-ber-er rung)
usherette, die Platzanweiserin (pluts-un-vise'-er-in)
waltz, der Walzer (vults'-er)

Do you play tennis (golf)? Spielen Sie Tennis (Golf)?

shpeel'-en zee ten'-iss, golf

I should like a game with you Ich möchte gern mit Ihnen spielen

ich murch'-ter gairn mit ee'-nen shpeel'-en

Have you brought your tennis-racket (golf-clubs)? Haben Sie Ihren Tennis-schläger (Ihre Golfschläger) mitgebracht?

hah'-ben zee ee'-ren ten'-iss-shlay-ger, ee'-rer golf'-shlay-ger mit'-geb-raCHt

Is there a tennis-court near? Gibt es einen Tennisplatz in der Nähe?

geebt ez i'-nen ten'-iss-pluts in dair nay'-er

Is this an eighteen-hole golf course? Ist das ein achtzehn Loch Golfplatz?

ist duss ine aCHt'-tsain loCH golf-pluts

Are the runs long (difficult) ist dee up-fahrt lung (shvee-rich)	Ist die Abfahrt lang (schwierig)
Would you care for a game of . . .? murcht'-en zee . . . shpeel'-en	Möchten Sie . . . spielen?
Is there riding (swimming) here? kun mun here rī'-ten (shvim'-en)	Kann man hier reiten (schwimmen)?
Where is the swimming-pool? vo ist duss shvim'-baht	Wo ist das Schwimmbad?
Can I have a cubicle? ich murch'-ter ī'-ner ka-bee'-ner hah'-ben	Ich möchte eine Kabine haben
Where can I hire a rowing-boat? vo kun ich ine roo'-der-boat mee'-ten	Wo kann ich ein Ruderboot mieten?
I should like to hire a sailing-boat (motor-boat) for this afternoon ich murch'-ter für hoy'-ter naCH'-mit-ahg ine zay'-gel-boat (mo-tōr-boat) mee'-ten	Ich möchte für heute nach-mittag ein Segelboot (Motor-boot) mieten
Where are the best ski slopes? vo ist duss best'-er shee'-gel-end-er	Wo ist das beste Skigelände?
How do we get there? vee komm'-en vere dort hin	Wie kommen wir dort hin?
Can we hire the equipment (boots, skis, sticks) here? kurn'-en vere dee owce-rust-ōōng'-en (shee'-shteef-el, shee'-er, shee'-sturk-er) here lie'-en	Können wir die Ausrüstungen, (Skistiefel, Skier, Skistöcke) hier leihen?
Where is the ice-rink? vo ist dee ice-bahn	Wo ist die Eisbahn?
Where can we skate here? vo kurn'-en vere here shlitt'-shoo lowf'-en	Wo können wir hier Schlitt-schuh laufen?
Are you going to the races? gay'-en zee tsōōm pfair'-der-ren-nen	Gehen Sie zum Pferderennen?

How do I get to the race-course ?	Wie komme ich zur Rennbahn?
	vee komm'-er ich tsoor renn'-bahn
Two tickets for the stand please	Zwei Tribünenplätze, bitte
	tsvī tree-bü'-nen-plets-er bitt'-er
Which is the favourite?	Welches ist der Favorit?
	velch'-es ist dair fah'-vo-reet
My horse was not even placed	Mein Pferd hatte noch nicht mal einen Platz
	mine pfaird hut'-er noCH nicht mahl i'-nen pluts
Two Marks to win on . . .	Zwei Mark auf . . . Gewinn
	tsvī mark owf . . . ger'-vinn
Three Marks each way on . . .	Drei Mark in jedem Fall auf . . .
	dry mark in yay'-dem full owf . .

Smoking is forbidden in cinemas as well as in theatres. Cinema performances are not continuous, so it is advisable to find out when the film starts and go in at the beginning.

There is a ball at the Casino on Saturday	Am Sonnabend ist ein Ball im Kasino
	um zonn-ah'-bent ist ine bul im kass'-ee-no
Should one wear evening dress?	Muss man Abendkleidung anziehen?
	mōōss mun ah'-bent-klī'-dōōng un'-tsee-en
Would you like to dance ?	Möchten Sie tanzen?
	murcht'-en zee tunts'-en
The band is excellent	Die Kapelle ist ausgezeichnet
	dee kup-ell'-er ist owce'-ge-tsīch-net
May I see you home ?	Darf ich Sie nach Hause begleiten?
	darf ich zee naCH how'-zer beg-lī'-ten
When shall I see you again ?	Wann sehe ich Sie wieder?
	vun zay'-er ich zee vee'-der

Do you know what is on at the cinema (theatre) ?	Wissen Sie was im Kino (Theater) gespielt wird ?

vis'-en zee vuss im keen'-o (tay-aht'-er) gesh-peelt' virt

What time does it start ?	Wann fängt es an ?

vunn fengt ez un

Two stalls, please	Zwei Parkettplätze bitte

tsvī park-ett'-plets-er bitt'-er

Two circle	Zwei erster Rang

tsvī airst'-er rung

We enjoyed the show very much	Uns hat die Vorstellung sehr gut gefallen

ōōns hut dee fore'-stell-ōōng zair goot ger-full'-en

CAMPING, HIKING AND WEATHER

Recognised camping sites are, in the main, extremely well organised and provide amenities such as drinking water, sanitary arrangements, showers, etc., and possibly a restaurant and/or shop, for a moderate charge per person per night.

VOCABULARY

air mattress, die Luftmatratze (lōōft'-mah-trats'-er)
bottle opener, der Flaschenöffner (flush'-en-öff-ner)
bucket, der Eimer (ī'-mer)
camp, to, zelten (tselt'-en)
camping site, der Zeltplatz (tselt'-pluts)
candle, die Kerze (kairts'-er)
caravan, der Wohnwagen (vohn-vah-gen)
clearing, die Lichtung (licht'-ōōng)
climb, to, besteigen (ber'-shtī-gen)
cold, kalt (kult)
cooking utensils, das Kochgeschirr (koCH'-ger-shirr)
cork-screw, der Korkenzieher (kork'-en-tsee-er)
country, das Land (lunt)
dawn, die Dämmerung (demm'-er-ōōng)
drinking water, das Trinkwasser (trink'-vuss'-er)
farm, der Bauernhof (bow'-ern-hōf)
farmer, der Bauer (bow'-er)
field, das Feld (felt)
forest, der Wald (vult)
frying-pan, die Bratpfanne (braht-pfunn'-er)
groundsheet, der Zeltboden (tselt'-bō'-den)
haversack, der Brotbeutel (broat-boy'-tel)

heat, die Hitze (hit'-ser)
hike, to, wandern (vunn'-dern)
hitch-hike, to, sich mitnehmen lassen (sich mit'-nay-men luss'-en)
hill, der Hügel (hüg'-el)
ice, das Eis (ice)
inn, das Gasthaus (gust-house)
lake, der See (zay)
lane, der Weg (vaig)
lightning, der Blitz (blits)
log, der Klotz (klöts)
matches, die Streichhölzer (shtrīch-hölts'-er)
methylated spirit, der Spiritus (shpee'-ri-tōōss)
mist, der Nebel (nay'-bel)
moss, das Moos (moss)
mountain, der Berg (bairg)
mountain pass, der Pass (pus')
paraffin, das Petroleum (pet-rohl-ee-ōōm)
path, der Pfad (pfaht)
penknife, das Taschenmesser (tush'-en-mess'-er)
picnic, to, im Freien essen (im fry' en ess'-en)
pole, der Pol (pole)
rain, der Regen (ray'-gen)
refuse, rubbish, der Abfall (up'-fall)
refuse bin, der Mülleimer (müll-ī'-mer)
river, der Fluss (flooss)
sandwich, das belegte Brot (ber' laygt'-er broat)
sauce-pan, der Kochtopf (koCH-topf)
shower, die Dusche (doosh'-er)
sleeping-bag, der Schlafsack (shlahf-zuck)
snow, der Schnee (shnay)
storm, der Sturm (shtōōrm)
stove, der Kocher (koCH'-er)
stream, der Strom (shtroam)
summit, der Gipfel (gip'-fel)
tent, das Zelt (tselt)
tent peg, der Zeltpflock (tselt-pflock)
thermos, die Thermosflasche (tair-moss-flush'-er)
thunderstorm, das Gewitter (ger'-vit'-er)
tighten the ropes, to, die Seile festmachen (dee zī'-ler fest-maCH'-en)
tin-opener, der Büchsenöffner (büx'-en-urf'-ner)
torch, die Taschenlampe (tush'-en-lump'-er)
valley, das Tal (tahl)
village, das Dorf (dörf)
waterfall, der Wasserfall (vuss'-er-full)
weather, das Wetter (vett'-er)
weather (bad), schlechtes Wetter (shlecht'-es vett'-er)
weather (good), gutes Wetter (goot'-es vett'-er)
wind, der Wind (vind)
wood, der Wald (vult)
youth hostel, die Jugendherberge (yōō'-gent hair-bair-ger)

We are looking for a camping site	Wir suchen einen Zeltplatz

vere zōōCH'-en i'-nen tselt-pluts

How far is it to . . . ?	Wie weit ist es zum . . . ?

vee vite ist ez tsōōm . .

Can we camp here for the night ?	Können wir hier für eine Nacht zelten ?

kurn'-en vere here für i'-ner naCHt tselt'-en

Where can we get drinking water ?	Wo können wir Trinkwasser bekommen ?

voh kurn'-en vere trink'-vuss-er ber'-komm-en

Where can I buy paraffin (methylated spirit) ?	Wo kann ich Petroleum (Spiritus) kaufen ?

voh kun ich pet-rohl-ee-ōōm (shpee'-ri-tōōss) kowf'-en

Is the next village (town) far from here ?	Ist das nächste Dorf (die nächste Stadt) weit von hier ?

ist duss next'-er dorf (dee next'-er shtutt) vite fon here

Can you give me a lift to . . . ?	Können Sie mich nach . . . mitnehmen ?

kurn'-en zee mich naCH . . . mit'-nay-men

We are lost	Wir haben uns verlaufen

vere hah'-ben ōōns fair'-lowf'-en

Can you show us the way to . . . ?	Können Sie uns den richtigen Weg nach . . . zeigen ?

kurn'-en zee ōōns dane rich-tich'-en vaig naCH . . . tsīg'-en

How far is it to the Youth Hostel ?	Wie weit ist es zur Jugend-herberge ?

vee vite ist ez tsoor yōō'-gent-hair-bair-ger

Keep straight on	Immer gerade aus

imm'-er ger-rah'-der owce

It is very cold (hot)	Es ist sehr kalt (heiss)

ez ist zair kult (hice)

It looks like rain	Es sieht nach Regen aus

ez zeet naCH ray'-gen owce

May we take shelter here ? — Können wir uns hier unter-stellen?

kur*n*'-en vere ŏŏns here ŏŏn'-ter-shtell-en

Can you recommend a cheap restaurant? — Können Sie eine billige Gaststätte empfehlen?

kur*n*'-en zee i'-ner bill'-ig-er gust-shtett'-er emp'-fay-len

Can we cut across country? — Können wir feldein gehen?

kur*n*'-en vere felt'-ine gay'-en

We want to keep to the main road — Wir wollen auf der Hauptstrasse bleiben

vere voll'-en owf dair howpt-shtrahss'-er bli'-ben

May we light a fire? — Dürfen wir ein Feuer an-machen?

dürf'-en vere ine foy'-er un-maCH'-en

Beware of the dog — Vorsicht, bissiger Hund!

for-sicht biss'-ich-er hŏŏnt

Save water — Wasser sparen

vuss'-er shpah'-ren

Put rubbish in the proper place — Abfälle in den Mülleimer!

up-fell'-er in dane müll-i'-mer

Do not disturb others — Nehmen Sie Rücksicht auf Andere

nay'-men zee rück'-zicht owf un'-der'-er

The ground is very damp after rain — Der Boden ist nach dem Regen sehr feucht

dair bo'-den ist naCH dame ray'-gen zair foy-cht

Is the ascent difficult? — Ist der Aufstieg schwierig?

ist dair owf'-shteeg shvee'-rich

You will need a guide — Sie müssen einen Führer haben

zee müss'-en i'-nen für'-er hah'-ben

The path is blocked by snow — Der Weg ist durch Schnee blockiert

dair vaig ist dŏŏrch sh'-nay block'-eert

The rocks are covered with ice — Die Felsen sind mit Eis bedeckt

dee fell'-zen zint mitt i*s* her'-deckt

The mist may come down suddenly	Der Nebel kommt ganz plötzlich

dair nay'-bel komt gunts plurts'-lich

There are often thunderstorms at this time of the year	In dieser Jahreszeit sind Gewitter sehr häufig

in dee'-zer yahr'-ez-tsite zint ger-vitt'-er zair hoy'-fich

The wind is getting up	Es wird sehr windig

ez virt zair vind'-ich

Do you know the weather forecast?	Haben Sie den Wetterbericht gehört?

hah'-ben zee dane vett'-er-ber-icht ger'-hurt

SHOPPING

In shops service is usually efficient, and in most shops one can find an assistant with some knowledge of English.

Sizes are marked differently from the British system, though this will often be understood. Clothing is measured in centimetres (1 inch is rather less than 2½ centimetres), and cloth is sold by the metre (1 metre is just under 40 inches). A German pound (weight) is roughly 10 per cent more than the British pound; a kilogram equals two German pounds.

SHOPKEEPERS AND SHOPS

	Shopkeeper	Shop
baker	der Bäcker (beck'-er)	die Bäckerei (beck'-er-ī)
bookshop	der Buchhändler (booCH'-hent-ler)	die Buchhandlung (booCH'-hunt-loong)
butcher	der Schlächter (shlecht'-er)	die Schlächterei (shlecht'-er-ī)
	or der Fleischer (fly'-sher)	die Fleischerei (fly'-sher-ī)
	or der Metzger (mets'-ger)	die Metzgerei (mets'-ger-ī)
cake-shop	der Konditor (kon'-dee-tor)	die Konditorei (kon'-dee-tor-ī)
chemist	der Drogist (dro-gist)	die Drogerie (dro-ger-ee)
	or der Apotheker (ah-po-tay'-ker)	die Apotheke (ah-po-tay'-ker)

cleaner		die Reinigung (ry-nee-goóng)
dyer		die Färberei (ferb'-er-ī)
dairy		das Milchgeschäft (milch-ger'-sheft)
delicatessen		das Delikatessengeschäft (day-lee-kah-tess'-en-ger-sheft)
department store		das Kaufhaus (kowf'-house)
draper	der Weisswarenhändler (vice'-vahr'-en-hend-ler)	die Weisswarenhandlung (vice'-vahr'-en-hunt'-lōōng)
fishmonger	der Fischhändler (fish'-hend-ler)	das Fischgeschäft (fish-ger'-sheft)
fruiterer	der Obst-und Gemüsehändler (ōbst-ōōnt ger'mü'-zer-hend-ler)	die Obst-und Gemüsehandlung (obst-ōōnt ger-mü'-zer-hunt'-lōōng)
grocer	der Kolonialhändler (ko-lo-nee-ahl-hend-ler)	die Kolonialhandlung (ko-lo-nee-ahl-hunt'-lōōng)
hairdresser	der Friseur (free-zur)	der Friseursalon (free-zur-zah-long)
ironmonger	der Eisenwarenhändler (ī'-zen-vahr'-en-hend-ler)	die Eisenwarenhandlung (ī'-zen-vahr'-en-hunt'-lōōng)
jeweller	der Juwelier (yōō'-vel-eer)	das Juwelengeschäft (yōō'-vale-n-ger'-sheft)
leather goods	der Lederwarenhändler (lay'-dair-vahr'-en-hend-ler)	die Lederwarenhandlung (lay'-dair-vahr'-en-hunt'-lōōng)
newsagent	der Zeitungshändler (tsi'-tōōngs-hend-ler) (also sells tobacco and cigarettes)	das Zeitungsgeschäft (tsi'-tōōngs-ger'-sheft)
perfumery		die Parfümerie (par-fü'-mer-ee)
photographic shop	der Photohändler (fo-to-hend'-ler)	das Photogeschäft (fo-to-ger'sheft)
shoemaker (repairs)	der Schuhmacher (shoo-maCH'-er)	die Schuhmacherei (shoo-maCH'-er-ī)
shoe-shop		das Schuhgeschäft (shoo-ger'-sheft)
stationer	der Papierhändler (pup'-eer-hend-ler)	die Papierhandlung (pup'-eer-hunt'-lōōng)
sweet-shop confectioner		die Konditorei (kon'-dee-tor ī)

POST OFFICE AND TELEPHONE

In the larger offices an official can usually be found who understands some English. Passports may be required for some services. In Germany and Switzerland letter-boxes are painted yellow and are frequently built flush into a wall, making them difficult to find at first. In Switzerland air-mail letters should be handed in at a post office; if put in a letter-box they will be sent by ordinary mail.

When telephoning, numbers are pronounced in twos, e.g. 50 41 85 would be Fünfzig einundvierzig fünfundachtzig. The figure 2 is often pronounced zwo (tsvo) instead of zwei, to save confusion with drei.

VOCABULARY

air-mail, die Luftpost (lōoft'-posst)
call (telephone), der Anruf (un'-roof)
call-box, der Münzenfernsprecher (münts'-en-fairn-shprech-er)
collection, die Leerung (lay'-rōong)
delivery, die Lieferung (lee'-fair-rōong)
directory (telephone), das Telephonbuch (tel-er-phone-booCH)
express, Eil . . . (ile . . .)
G.P.O., die Hauptpost (howpt'-posst)
international money order, die internationale Postanweisung (in'-ter-nah-tee-ō-nahl'-er posst'-un-vī-zōong)
letter, der Brief (brief)
parcel, das Paket (puck-ate')
post-card, die Postkarte (posst-kart'-er)
post-man, der Postbote (posst-boat'-er)
post office, das Postamt (posst'-umt)
postal order ⎫
money order ⎭ die Postanweisung (posst'-un-vī-zōong)
register, to, einschreiben (ine'-shrī-ben)
reply paid, Antwort bezahlt (ant'-vōrt ber'-tsahlt)
stamp, die Briefmarke (brief'-mark'-er)
telegram, das Telegramm (tel-ay-grumm')
telephone, to, telephonieren (tel-er-phone-eer'-en)
telephone, der Fernsprecher (fairn'-shprech-er)
trunk-call, das Ferngespräch (fairn'-gesh-prech)

Which is the way to the post office ? Wie komme ich zum Postamt ?

vee komm'-er ch tsōōm posst'-umt

I want stamps, please Ich möchte Briefmarken bitte

ich murcht'-er brief'-mark-en bitt'-er

How much are letters (post-cards) for abroad ?	Was kosten Briefe (Post-karten) ins Ausland?
	vuss kost'-en brief'-er (posst'-kart-en) inz owce'-lunt
Will this go tonight ?	Geht das heute abend fort?
	gate duss hoy'-ter ah'-bent fort
This is to go air-mail	Das soll mit Luftpost gehen
	duss zoll mit looft'-posst gay'-en
I want to register this letter (parcel)	Ich möchte diesen Brief (dieses Paket) per Einschreiben schicken
	ich murcht'-er dee'-zen brief (dee'-zez puck-ate') perr ine'-shri-ben shick'-en
Which window do I go to ?	Zu welchem Schalter muss ich gehen?
	tsoo vellch'-em shult'-er mooss ich gay'-en
Will this go letter post ?	Geht das als Brief?
	gate duss ulce brief
I want to send a telegram	Ich möchte ein Telegramm auf-geben
	ich murch'-ter ine tel-ay-grumm' owf'-gay-ben
This is for abroad	Dies ist fürs Ausland
	deess ist fürz owce'-lunt
Where do I cash money orders?	Wo bekommt man Postan-weisungen ausgezahlt?
	voh bek-ommt' mun posst'-un-vi-zoong-en owce'-get-sahlt
Where is the Poste Restante ?	Wo sind postlagernde Briefe?
	voh zint posst'-lahg'-ern-der brief'-er
Are there any letters for me in the Poste Restante ?	Sind postlagernde Briefe für mich da?
	zint posst'-lahg'-ern-der brief'-er für mich dah
I want to telephone	Ich möchte telephonieren
	ich murch'-ter tel-er-phone-eer'-en
Who is speaking ?	Wer ist da?
	vair ist dah
This is . . .	Hier ist . . .
	here ist

Can I speak to . . . ?	Kann ich . . . sprechen ?
	kun ich . . . shprech'-en
Operator !	Fräulein!
	froy'-line
Wrong number	Falsche Verbindung
	fulsh'-er fair-bin'-dŏŏng
Will you get me . . . please ?	Bitte, verbinden Sie mich mit . . .?
	bitt'-er, fair-bin'-den zee mich mit . . .
How much do I owe you for the call ?	Was bin ich Ihnen für das Gespräch schuldig?
	vuss bin ich ee'-nen fur duss gesh-prech shool'-dig

CHEMIST AND HAIRDRESSER

VOCABULARY

aspirin, das Aspirin (a-spi-reen')
bathsalts, das Badesalz (bahd'-er-zults)
bandage, der Verband (fair-bunt)
bandage (crêpe), der Kreppverband (krepp'-fair-bunt)
bleach, to, bleichen (blī'-chen)
castor oil, das Rizinusöl (ree'-tsin-ooss-url)
colour rinse, die Farbwäsche (fahrb-vesh'-er)
comb, der Kamm (kum)
cosmetics, Schönheitsmittel (shurn'-hīts-mitt'-el)
cotton-wool, die Watte (vutt'-er)
curlers, Lockenwickler (lock'-en-vick-ler)
dryer, der Föhn (furn)
eau de cologne, Kölnisch Wasser (kurl'-nish vuss'-er)
eyebrow pencil, der Augenbrauenstift (owg'-en-brow'-en-shtift)
face cream, Hautcrème (howt'-craim)
gargle, das Mundwasser (moont'-vuss-er)
hair grip, die Haarklemme (hahr'-klemm'-er)
hair lacquer, Haarlack (hahr'-luck)
hairnet, das Haarnetz (hahr-nets)
hair-pin, die Haarnadel (hahr-nahd'-el)
hair-oil, das Haaröl (hahr'-url)
hair slide, die Haarklemme (hahr-klemm'-er)
laxative, das Abführmittel (up'-für-mitt-el)
lint, der Verbandstoff (fair-bunt'-shtoff)
lipstick, der Lippenstift (lip'-en-shtift)
mirror (pocket), der Taschenspiegel (tush' en shpeeg' gel)
nail file, die Nagelfeile (nahg'-el fi '-ler)

nail brush, die Nagelbürste (nahg'-el-bürst'-er)
nail varnish, Nagellack (nahg'-el-luck)
nail varnish remover, Nagellackentferner (nahg'-el-luck-ent-fern'-er)
ointment, die Salbe (zulb'-er)
perfume, das Parfüm (par'-füm)
plaster, das Pflaster (pflust'-er)
powder compact, die Puderdose (poo'-der-do'-zer)
powder (medicinal), das Pulver (pool'-fer)
powder (face), das Puder (poo'-der)
powder puff, die Puderquaste (poo'-der-k-vusst'-er)
prescription, das Rezept (ray-tsept)
pumice-stone, der Bimsstein (bimss'-shtine)
razor blades, die Rasierklingen (rah-zeer'-kling'-en)
sanitary towels, die Binden (bin'-den)
shampoo, das Haarwaschmittel (hahr-vush'-mitt'-el)
shampoo and set, Waschen und Legen (vush'-en öönt lay'-gen)
shaving brush, der Rasierpinsel (rah-zeer'-pin-zel)
shaving lotion, das Rasierwasser (rah-zeer'-vuss'-er)
shaving soap, die Rasierseife (rah-zeer'-zī'-fer)
sleeping tablets, die Schlaftabletten (shlahf'-ta-blett'-en)
soap, die Seife (zī'-fer)
sponge, der Schwamm (shvumm)
sunglasses, die Sonnenbrille (zonn'-en-brill-er)
suntan oil, das Sonnenöl (zonn'-en-url)
toilet-paper, das Toilettenpapier (twa-lett'-en-pup-eer)
talcum powder, Talkum (tal'-köóm)
throat pastilles, Halspastillen (hulce-past'-ill'-en)
tooth-brush, die Zahnbürste (tsahn'-bürst'-er)
tooth-paste, die Zahnpasta (tsahn'-pust'-ah)
wave (permanent), die Dauerwelle (dow'-er-vell'-er)
wave set, die Wasserwelle (vuss'-er-vell'-er)

Can you recommend me a good hairdresser ?

Können Sie mir einen guten Friseur empfehlen?

kurn'-nen zee mere i'-nen goot'-en free-zur' emp-fay'-len

I would like to make an appointment for . . .

Ich möchte mich für . . . anmelden

ich murcht'-er mich für . . . un'-meld'-en

I should like a haircut

Ich möchte mir die Haare schneiden lassen

ich murcht'-er mere dee hahr'-er shnī'-den luss'-en

Shampoo and set, please

Waschen und Legen, bitte

vush'-en öönt lay'-gen bitt'-er

When can I come ?	Wann soll ich kommen?
	vunn zoll ich komm'-en
I should prefer tomorrow morning (Thursday)	Ich möchte lieber morgen früh (Donnerstag) kommen
	ich murcht'-er lee'-ber morg'-en früh (donn'-ers-tahg) komm'-en
I want a permanent wave	Ich möchte Dauerwelle haben
	ich murcht'-er dow'-er-vell-er hah'-ben
With waves and curls	Mit Wellen und Locken
	mit vell'-en oont lock'-en
Not too short	Nicht zu kurz
	nicht tsoo koorts
Quite short	Ganz kurz
	gunts koorts
Don't cut any off the top	Schneiden Sie nichts von oben ab
	shni'-den zee nichts fon o'-ben up
Just trim it round the sides and back	Schneiden Sie nur an den Seiten und hinten
	shni'-den zee noor un dane zi'-ten oont hin'-ten
The water is too hot	Das Wasser ist zu heiss
	duss vuss'-er ist tsoo hiss
The dryer is too hot; can you adjust it?	Der Föhn ist zu heiss; können Sie ihn bitte regulieren?
	dair furn ist tsoo hice, kurn'-en zee een bitt'-er ray'-goo-lee-ren
I would like some lacquer (oil)	Ich möchte etwas Lack (Öl)
	ich murcht'-er et-vuss luck (url)
Could you give me a colour rinse ?	Ich möchte mein Haar getönt haben
	ich murcht'-er mine hahr ger'-turnt hah-ben
That is very nice	Das ist sehr nett
	duss ist sair net
I want my nails manicured	Ich möchte meine Nägel manikürt haben
	ich murcht'-er mi'-ner nay-gel mah-nee-kürt hah'-ben

Can I have something to read? Kann ich etwas zum Lesen haben?

kun ich et'-vuss tsōōm lay'-zen hah'-ben

Can you make up an English prescription ? Können Sie ein englisches Rezept herstellen?

kurn'-en zee ine eng'-lish-ez ray-tsept hair'-shtell-en

Please make up this prescription Bitte machen Sie dieses Rezept

bitt'-er maCH'-en zee dee'-zez ray-tsept

I shall call for it later Ich werde es später abholen

ich vair'-der ez shpate'-er up'-ho-len

Can you give me something for constipation (diarrhoea, headache) ? Können Sie mir etwas für Verstopfung (Durchfall, Kopfschmerzen) geben?

kurn'-en zee mere et'-vuss fur fair-shtopf'-ōōng (dōōrch'-fal, kopf'-shmair-tsen) gay'-ben

I have a bad cold (cold in my chest) Ich habe einen schweren Schnupfen (eine Brusterkältung)

ich hah'-ber ĭ'-nen shvair'-en shnōōp'-fen (ĭ'-ner brōost-air-kelt-ōōng)

I have blisters Ich habe Blasen

ich hah'-ber blah'-zen

Can you give me something for insect (mosquito) bites ? Können Sie mir etwas gegen Insekten- (Mücken-) stiche geben?

kurn'-nen zee mere et'-vuss gay-gen in-zekt'-en (mück'-en) shtich'-er gay'-ben

My back is badly sunburnt Ich habe Sonnenbrand im Rücken

ich hah'-ber zonn'-en-brunt im rük'-en

Can you give me something to rub on it ? Können Sie mir etwas zum Einreiben geben?

kurn'-en zee mere et'-vuss tsōōm ine'-rī-ben gay'-ben

Directions for use Gebrauchsanweisung

ge / brọwCHs-un-vī-zōōng

N.B.—See also under Accident and Illness, page 106.

PHOTOGRAPHY

VOCABULARY

camera, die Kamera (kum′-er-ah)
camera (movie), die Filmkamera (film-kum′-er-ah)
develop, to, entwickeln (ent-vick′-eln)
enlarge, to, vergrössern (fair-grurss′-ern)
film, der Film (film)
film (colour), der Farbfilm (farb′-film)
film winder, das Filmwickler (film-vick′-ler)
filter, der Filter (fil′-ter)
lens, die Linse (lin′-zer)
lens-hood, die Linsenkappe (lin′-zen-kupp′-er)
light-meter, der Belichtungsmesser (ber′-licht′-ŏŏngs-mess′-er)
negative, das Negativ (nay′-gah-teef)
print, der Abzug (up′-tsoog)
range-finder, der Entfernungsmesser (ent′-fair-nŏŏngs-mess′-er)
shutter, der Verschluss (fair-shlŏŏss)
view-finder, der Sucher (zooCH′-er)

I want some films for my camera	Ich möchte Filme für meine Kamera
	ich murcht′-er film′-er für mī′-ner kum′-er-ah
Have you colour films?	Haben Sie Farbfilme?
	hah′-ben zee farb′-film-er
Have you any fast (fine grain) film?	Haben Sie einen schnellen (Feinkorn) Film?
	hah′-ben zee ī′-nen shnell′-en (fine-korn) film
Do you develop films?	Entwickeln Sie Filme?
	ent-vick′-eln zee film′-er
One print of each	Je einen Abzug
	yay ī′-nen up′-tsoog
On shiny (matt) paper	Auf Glanzpapier (mattem Papier)
	owf glunts′-pup-eer′ (mutt′-em pup-eer′)
When will they be ready?	Wann werden sie fertig sein?
	vunn vair′-den zee fair′-tich zine

I want them as soon as possible — Ich möchte sie möglichst bald haben

ich murcht'-er zee murg'-lichst bult hah'-ben

Please enlarge these two — Bitte vergrössern Sie diese beiden

bitt'-er fair-grurss'-ern zee dee'-zer bī'-den

Can you repair my camera for me ? — Können Sie mir die Kamera reparieren?

kurn'-en zee mere dee kum'-er-ah rep-ar-eer'-en

The shutter does not work — Der Verschluss funktioniert nicht

dair fair-shlōōss' fōōnk-tsee-on-eert' nicht

The film does not wind properly — Der Film dreht sich nicht richtig

dair film drait sich nicht rich'-tich

Can you put the film in the camera please? — Können Sie den Film in die Kamera einlegen?

kurn'-en zee dane film in dee kum'-er-a ine'-lay'-gen

I dropped it — Ich habe sie fallen lassen

ich hah'-ber zee fal'-en luss'-en

Can you have it ready for this evening ? — Können Sie es bis heute abend machen?

kurn'-en zee ez biss hoy'-ter ah'-bent maCH'-en

They are under-exposed (over-exposed) — Sie sind unterbelichtet (überbelichtet)

zee zint ōōnt'-er-ber'-licht'-et (ü'-ber-ber'-licht'-et)

MISCELLANEOUS

VOCABULARY

battery, die Batterie (but'-er-ee)
big, gross (grōss)
book, das Buch (booCH)
bracelet, das Armband (ahrm-bunt)
brooch, die Brosche (brōsh'-er)
button, der Knopf (knopf)
cheap, billig (bill'-ich)

cigarette, die Zigarette (tsi-gar-ett'-er)
cigar, die Zigarre (tsi'-gar'-er)
collar stud, der Kragenknopf (krahg'-en-knopf)
cotton, die Baumwolle (bowm'-voll'-er)
cuff links, Manschettenknöpfe (mun-shett'-en-knurpf-er)
dear, teuer (toy'-er)
dictionary, das Wörterbuch (vurt'-er-booCH)
disinfectant, das Desinfektionsmittel (des-in-fect-ee-owns-mitt'-el)
doll, die Puppe (pŏŏ'-per)
earrings, die Ohrringe (ōhr'-ring-er)
envelopes, Briefumschläge (brief-ŏŏm'-shlay-ger)
elastic, das Gummiband (goom-ee-bunt)
gramophone record, die Schallplatte (shul'-plutt-er)
guide-book, das Reisehandbuch (rī'- zer-hunt-booCH)
ink, die Tinte (tint'-er)
invisible mending, Kunststopfen (koonst-shtopf'-en)
label, das Etikette (ay-tee-kett')
lace, die Spitzen (shpits'-en)
large, gross (grōss)
lighter, das Feuerzeug (foy'-er tsoyg)
lighter flint, der Feuerstein (foy'-er-shtine)
lighter fuel, Benzin (ben'-tseen)
long, lang (lung)
magazine, die Zeitschrift (tsite-shrift)
map, die Landkarte (lunt-kart'-er)
matches, die Streichhölzer (shtrīch'-hurl-tser)
material, der Stoff (shtoff)
narrow, schmal (shmahl)
necklace, die Kette (kett'-er)
needle, die Nähnadel (nay'-nahd-el)
newspaper, die Zeitung (tsī-tŏŏng)
pen (ball-point), der Kugelschreiber (koog-el-shrīb'-er)
pen (fountain), der Füllfederhalter (füll-fay'-der-hult'-er)
pencil, der Bleistift (blī'-shtift)
pin, die Stecknadel (shteck'-nahd'-el)
pipe, die Pfeife (pfī'-fer)
pipe-cleaner, der Pfeifenreiniger (pfī'-fen-rī-nig-er)
plan, der Plan (Plahn)
purse, die Geldbörse (gelt-burs'-er)
refill, Ersatzfüllung (air-zuts'-fü-lŏŏng)
ribbon, das Band (bunt)
ring, der Ring (ring)
safety pin, die Sicherheitsnadel (zeech'-er-hītes-nahd-el)
sale, Verkauf (fair-kowf')
scissors, die Schere (shay'-rer)
self-service, Selbstbedienung (zelbst-ber'-dee-nŏŏng)
shoe-laces, die Schnürsenkel (shnür'-zenk'-el)
shoe polish, der Schuhcrème (shoo-craim)
short, kurz (kŏŏrts)
shop, das Geschäft (gesh-eft')

shop assistant, die Verkäuferin (fair-koy'-fair'-in)
silk, die Seide (zī'-der)
size, die Grösse (grurss'-er)
small, klein (kline)
soap powder, das Seifenpulver (zī'-fen-pool'-fer)
souvenir, das Andenken (un-denk-en)
spade, der Spaten (shpaht'-en)
spectacles, die Brille (brill'-er)
stick, der Stock (shtŏck)
strap, der Riemen (ree'-men)
string, der Bindfaden (bint'-fahd'-en)
suitcase, der Koffer (koff'-er)
thick, dick (dick)
thin, dünn (dünn)
thread (cotton), das Nähgarn (nay-garn)
tobacco, der Tabak (tah-buk')
toy, das Spielzeug (shpeel-tsoyg)
umbrella, der Schirm (sheerm)
wallet, die Brieftasche (brief-tush'-er)
watch, die Uhr (oor)
waterproof (adj.), wasserdicht (vuss'-er-dicht)
wide, weit (vite)
wool, die Wolle (voll'-er)
writing-paper, das Briefpapier (brief-pup-eer)
zip-fastener, der Reissverschluss (rice'-fair-shlōōss)

I want to buy . . .	Ich möchte . . .
	ich murcht'-er . . .
Do you sell . . . ?	Haben Sie . . . ?
	hah'-ben zee . . .
This is not my size	Das ist nicht meine Grösse
	duss ist nicht mī'-ner grurss'-er
Where is the market ?	Wo ist der Markt?
	vo ist dair mahr-kt
That is not what I want	Das ist nicht was ich möchte
	duss ist nicht vuss ich murcht'-er
I do not like the colour	Die Farbe gefällt mir nicht
	dee far'-ber gef-ellt' mere nicht
I prefer a darker (lighter) colour	Ich möchte eine dunklere (hellere) Farbe haben
	ich murcht'-er i'-ner dōōnk'-ler-er (hell' er-er) far'-ber hah'-ben

Have you anything bigger (smaller)?	Haben Sie etwas Grösseres (Kleineres)?
	hah'-ben zee et-vuss grurss'-er-ez (kline'-er-ez)
That is too dear	Das ist zu teuer
	duss ist tsoo toy'-er
Is that the cheapest you have?	Ist das das Billigste, das Sie haben?
	ist duss duss bill'-ich-ster, duss zee hah'-ben
I want a better quality	Ich möchte eine bessere Qualität
	ich murch'-ter i'-ner bess'-er-er k-vul-ee-tait
Have you nothing better?	Haben Sie nichts Besseres?
	hah'-ben zee nichts bess'-er-ez
I prefer something in silk (wool, cotton, nylon)	Ich würde etwas in Seide (Wolle, Baumwolle, Nylon) vorziehen
	ich vürd'-er et'-vuss in zi'-der (voll'-er, bowm'-voll'-er, nylon) for-tsee-en
Have you a carrier bag?	Haben Sie eine Tüte?
	hah'-ben zee i'-ner tü'-ter
That's exactly what I want	Das ist genau was ich wollte
	duss ist ger'-now vuss ich vollt'-er
Can you match this colour?	Haben Sie diese gleiche Farbe
	hah'-ben zee dee'-zer glich'-er fahrb'-er
It is broken (torn, stained)	Es ist entzwei (zerrissen, beschmutzt)
	ez ist ent'-tsvi (tsair'-riss-en, ber'-shmootst)
It does not fit me	Es passt mir nicht
	ez pusst mere nicht
Here is my address	Hier ist meine Adresse
	here ist mi'-ner ad'-dress'-er
I have not received ...	Ich habe ... nicht erhalten
	ich hah'-ber ... nicht air-hull'-ten
What do you charge for making one?	Was kostet es wenn Sie es anfertigen?
	vuss kost'-et ez, venn zee ez un'-fair-tig-en

When could I have it ? Wann könnte ich es haben?
vunn kurn'-ter ich ez hah'-ben

I will take it with me Ich nehme es mit
ich nay'-mer ez mit

Can you order it for me ? Können Sie es für mich bestellen?
kurn'-en zee ez für mich ber-shtell'-en

Can you wrap it up for me ? Würden Sie es bitte für mich
einpacken?
vürd'-en zee ez bitt'-er für mich ine-puck'-en

Please send it to this address Bitte schicken Sie es an diese
Adresse
bitt'-er shick'-en zee ez un dee' zer ad'-dress'-er

I will pay on delivery Ich werde bei Lieferung zahlen
ich vair'-der by leef-er-ōōng tsahl'-en

How much is it altogether ? Was macht es zusammen?
vuss maCHt es tsoo-zum'-en

Pay at the cash-desk, please Zahlen Sie bitte an der Kasse
tsahl'-en zee bitt'-er un dair kuss'-er

I bought this two days ago Ich habe es vor zwei Tagen
gekauft
ich hah'-ber ez fore tsvī tahg'-en ger'-kowft

It doesn't work Es geht nicht
ez gayt nicht

Can you change it ? Kann ich es umtauschen?
kun ich ez ōōm'-towsh-en

Have you English (American, Turkish) cigarettes ? Haben Sie englische (amerik-
anische, türkische) Zigar-
etten?
hah'-ben zee eng'-lish-er (um-air-ik-ahn'-ish-er, türk'-ish-er) tsi-gar-ett'-en

REPAIRS

I need new soles (heels) — Ich brauche neue Sohlen (Absätze)

ich browCH'-*er* noy'-*er* zō'-len (up'-zets-*er*)

When will they be ready ? — Wann werden sie fertig sein?

vunn vair'-den zee fair'-tich zine

I have broken my glasses — Meine Brille ist kaputt

mī'-ner brill'-er ist ka-pōōt'

I need a new lens (frame, bridge) — Ich brauche ein neues Glas (eine Fassung, einen Steg)

ich browCH-er ine noy'-ez gluss, (ī'-ner fuss'-ōōng, ī'-nen shtaig)

That is too tight (slack) — Das ist zu fest (lose)

duss ist tsoo fest (lo'-zer)

I want some dark glasses made with the same lenses — Ich möchte dunkle Gläser in derselben Schärfe haben.

ich murcht'-er dōōnk'-ler glay'-zer in dair-zelb'-en sherf'-er nah'-ben

My watch has stopped (is broken) — Meine Uhr ist stehengeblieben (ist kaputt)

mī'-ner oor ist shtay'-en-geb-lee'-ben, (ist ka-pōōt)

My watch needs cleaning — Meine Uhr muss gereinigt werden

mī'-ner oor mōōss ger-ī-nicht vair'-den

It gains (loses) — Sie geht vor (nach)

zee gate fore (naCH)

Please regulate it — Bitte regulieren Sie sie

bitt'-er reg-oo-leer'-en zee zee

The spring is broken — Die Feder ist kaputt

dee fay'-der ist ka-pōōt'

I overwound it — Ich habe sie überdreht

ich hah'-ber zee ü-ber-drait'

Give me a new strap, please — Geben Sie mir ein neues Band bitte

gay'-ben zee mere ine noy'-ez bunt bitt-'er

The lock on my case is broken	Das Schloss an meinem Koffer ist kaputt
	duss shloss un mī'-nem koff'-er ist ka-pōōt
Can you mend it ?	Können Sie es reparieren?
	kurn'-en zee ez rep-ar-eer'-en
How long will it take ?	Wie lange wird es dauern?
	vee lung'-er virt ez dow'-ern
Can you have it ready for this evening ?	Können Sie es bis heute abend machen?
	kurn'-en zee ez biss hoy'-ter ah'-bent maCH'-en
When shall I collect it ?	Wann soll ich es abholen?
	vunn zoll ich ez up'-hole-en
How much will it be ?	Wieviel wird es kosten?
	vee-feel virt ez kost'-en

COLOURS

beige, beige (*bay' sh*)
black, schwarz (*shvarts*)
blue, blau (*blow*)
brown, braun (*brown*)
dark, dunkel (*dōōnk'-el*)
emerald, smaragd (*smah'-rahkt*)
fawn, rehbraun (*ray-brown*)
green, grün (*grün*)
grey, grau (*grow*)
ivory, elfenbein (*elf'-en-bine*)
light, hell (*hell*)
mauve, hellviolett (*hell-vee-o-lett'*)
orange, orange (*o-runk'-she*)
pink, rosa (*roh-zah*)
plain, self-coloured, einfarbig (*ine-fahrb'-ich*)
red, rot (*rote*)
violet, violett (*vee-o-lett'*)
white, weiss (*vice*)
yellow, gelb (*gelp*)

CLOTHES

belt, der Gürtel (*gürt'-el*)
blouse, die Bluse (*bloo' zer*)
braces, die Hosenträger (*ho'-zen-tray-ger*)
brassière, der Büstenhalter (*büz'-ten-hult-er*)

cap, die Mütze (müt′-ser)
clothes, die Bekleidung (ber′-klī-dōōng)
coat, der Mantel (mun′-tel)
collar, der Kragen (krahg′-en)
dress, das Kleid (klite)
fur, der Pelz (pelts)
girdle, der Strumpfgürtel (shtrōōmpf′-gürt′-el)
gloves, die Handschuhe (hunt′-shoo′-er)
handkerchief, das Taschentuch (tush-en-tooCH)
hat, der Hut (hoot)
headsquare, das Kopftuch (kopf′-tooCH)
heel, der Absatz (up′-zahts)
jumper (as in English)
nightdress, das Nachthemd (naCHt′-hemt)
nylons, die Nylons (nylons)
pants, die Schlüpfer (shlüp′-fair)
petticoat, der Unterrock (ōōn′-ter-rock)
pullover, der Pullover (as in English)
pyjamas, der Schlafanzug (shlahf′-un-tsoog)
raincoat, der Regenmantel (ray′ gen-munt-el)
sandals, die Sandalen (zun′-dahl′-en)
shawl, der Schal (shahl)
shirt, das Hemd (hemt)
shoes, die Schuhe (shoo′-er)
skirt, der Rock (rock)
slip, der Unterrock (ōōn′-ter-rock)
slippers, die Hausschuhe (house-shoo-er)
socks, die Socken (zock′-en)
stockings, die Strümpfe (shtrümpf′-er)
suit (man's), der Anzug (un-tsoog)
suit (woman's), das Kostüm (kost′-üm)
suspender, der Strumpfhalter (strōōmpf′-hult-er)
tie, die Krawatte (kra-vat′-er)
trousers, die Hose (ho′-zer)
vest, das Unterhemd (ōōn′-ter-hemt)

The English size is . . .   Die englische Grösse ist . . .

dee eng′-lish′-er grurss′-er ist . . .

It is too big (small, broad,   Es ist zu gross (klein, weit,
narrow, tight)   schmal, eng)

ez ist tsoo gröss (kline, vite, shmahl, eng)

May I try this on?   Darf ich das anprobieren?

darf ich duss un′-pro-beer-en

It does not fit me   Es passt nicht

ez pusst nicht

Can you take it in at the waist ?	Können Sie es an der Taille enger machen?

kurn'-en zee ez un dair tî'-yer eng'-er maCH'-en

The heels are too high	Die Absätze sind zu hoch

dee up'-zets'-er zint tsoo hoCH

I want a beach outfit	Ich möchte eine Strandausrüstung

ich murcht'-er î'-ner shtrunt-owce'-rüst-ōōng

I would like to see some hand-embroidered . . .	Ich möchte einige handgestickte . . . sehen

ich murcht'-er î'-nig-er hunt-ger-shtickt'-er . . . zay'-en

I am looking for a dress with a round (low-cut) neck	Ich suche ein Kleid mit einem runden (tiefen) Ausschnitt

ich zooCH'-er îné klîte mit î'-nem rōōnt'-en (teef'-en) owce-shnitt

Where can I have this cleaned ?	Wo kann ich es reinigen lassen?

voh kun ich ez rî'-nee-gen luss'-en

Is there a laundry near here?	Gibt es eine Wäscherei in der Nähe?

geebt ez î'-ner vesh'-er-î in dair nay'-er

Can you proof this for me please?	Können Sie es wasserdicht machen bitte

kurn'-en zee ez vuss'-er-dicht maCH'-en bitt'-er

How long will it take?	Wie lange wird es dauern

vee lung'-er virt ez dow'-ern

FOOD

For main vocabulary see under RESTAURANTS, *page 36.*

bitter chocolate, die bittere Schokolade (bitt'-er-er shock-o-lahd'-er)
chocolate, die Schokolade (shock-o-lahd'-er)
fruit, das Obst (ōbst)
liqueur chocolates, die Likörpralinen (lee-kur-prahl'-een-en)
milk chocolate, die Milchschokolade (milch-shock-o-lahd'-er)
peppermints, die Pfefferminze (pfeff'-er-min-tser)
sweets, die Süssigkeiten (züss-ig-kite-en)
toffees, die Sahnenbonbons (zahn'-en-bong-bongs)

I want a pound (kilo) of . . .	Ich möchte ein Pfund (Kilo) . . . haben

ich murcht'-er ine pfŏŏnt (kilo) . . . hah'-ben

How much per pound ?	Wieviel kostet das Pfund?

vee'-feel kost'-et duss pfŏŏnt

Give me a bottle of milk	Geben Sie mir bitte eine Flasche Milch

gay-ben zee mere bitt'-er i'-ner flush'-er milch

I want a mature cheese	Ich möchte einen reifen Käse

ich murcht'-er i'-nen ri'-fen kay'-zer

Are these . . . ripe (fresh)	Sind diese . . . reif (frisch)

zint dee'-zer . . . rife (frish)

ACCIDENT AND ILLNESS

If involved in a traffic accident, it is advisable to ask for an interpreter when dealing with the police, as inability to express oneself in German might lead to misunderstandings and consequent delays.

VOCABULARY

PARTS OF THE BODY

ankle, der Knöchel (k-nurch'-el)
arm, der Arm (arm)
back, das Kreuz (kroyts)
blood, das Blut (bloot)
body, der Körper (kurp'-er)
bone, der Knochen (k-noch'-en)
bowel, der Darm (darm)
cheek, die Wange (vung'-er)
chest, die Brust (broost)
chin, das Kinn (kin)
ear, das Ohr (ore)
elbow, der Ellbogen (el'-boh-gen)
eye, das Auge (owg'-er)
eyelid, das Augenlid (ow'-gen-leed)
face, das Gesicht (ger'-zicht)
false teeth, das Gebiss (ger'-biss)
finger, der Finger (fing'-er)
foot, der Fuss (fooss)
gum, das Zahnfleisch (tsahn'-flīsh)
hand, die Hand (hunt)

head, der Kopf (kopf)
heart, das Herz (hairts)
heel, der Hacken (huck'-en)
hip, die Hüfte (hüft'-er)
jaw, der Kiefer (kee'-fer)
joint, das Gelenk (ger'-lenk')
kidney, die Niere (nee'-rer)
knee, das Knie (k-nee)
knee-cap, die Kniescheibe (k-nee-shī'-ber)
leg, das Bein (bine)
lip, die Lippe (lip'-er)
liver, die Leber (lay'-ber)
lung, die Lunge (loong'-er)
mouth, der Mund (moont)
muscle, die Muskel (moos'-kel)
neck, der Hals (hulce)
nerve, der Nerv (nairf)
nose, die Nase (nah'-zer)
shoulder, die Schulter (shool'-ter)
skin, die Haut (howt)
stomach, der Magen (mahg'-en)
throat, der Hals (hulce)
toe, die Zehe (tsay'-er)
tongue, die Zunge (tsoong'-er)
tooth, der Zahn (tsahn)
wrist, das Handgelenk (hunt-ger'-lenk')

GENERAL

abscess, das Geschwür (ger'-shvür)
accident, der Unfall (ōōn'-fal)
ambulance, der Krankenwagen (krunk'-en-vahg'-en)
appendicitis, die Blinddarmentzündung (blint-dahrm-ent-tsün-dōong)
bandage, der Verband (fair-bunt')
bite, der Biss (biss)
blister, die Blase (blah'-zer)
boil, die Beule (boy'-ler)
bruise, die Quetschung (kvett'-shōong)
burn, die Brandwunde (brunt'-vōōnd'-er)
    heart-burn, Sodbrennen (zote'-brenn'-en)
    sun-burn, Sonnenbrand (zonn'-en-brunt)
chemist, die Apotheke (up-ō-tay'-ker)
chill, die Erkältung (air-kelt-ōōng)
chiropodist, der Fusspfleger (fooss-pflayg-er)
cold, die Erkältung (air-kelt-ōōng)
constipation, Verstopfung (fair-shtopf'-ōōng)
consulting room, das Sprechzimmer (shprech'-tsimm'-er)
convalescence, die Genesung (ger'-nay-sōong)
convulsions, der Krampf (krumpf)
corn, das Hühnerauge (hü'-ner-owg'-er)

cough, der Husten (hōōs'-ten)
cramp, der Krampf (krampf)
cure, das Heilmittel, die Kur (hile-mitt'-el, koor)
cut, scratch, der Schnitt, die Schramme (shnitt', shrumm'-er)
dentist, der Zahnarzt (tsahn'-artst)
diarrhoea, der Durchfall (doorch'-fal)
diet, die Diät (dee-ate')
doctor, der Arzt (artst)
emergency service, der Notdienst (note-deenst)
epidemic, die Epidemie (ay-pee-de-mee)
faint, to, ohnmächtig werden (ohn'-mech-tich vaird'-en)
fever, das Fieber (fee-ber)
filling (stopping), die Plombe (plom'-ber)
fracture, der Knochenbruch (k-noch'-en-brooCH)
hay-fever, der Heuschnupfen (hoy'-shnoōp'-fen)
headache, die Kopfschmerzen (kopf'-shmair-tsen)
health, die Gesundheit (ger'-zoont-hīte)
hospital, das Krankenhaus (krunk'-en-house)
illness, die Krankheit (krunk'-hite)
indigestion, die Verdauungsstörung (fair-dow-ōōngs-shtur'-ōōng)
infection, die Ansteckung (un-shtek'-ōōng)
influenza, die Grippe (grip'-er)
injury, die Verletzung (fair-lets-ōōng)
insomnia, Schlaflosigkeit (shlahf-lo-sich-kite)
interpreter, der Dolmetscher (dol'metsh-er)
measles, die Masern (mah'-zern)
nausea, die Übelkeit (ü'-bel-kite)
nerve, der Nerv (nairf)
nurse, die Pflegerin (pflay'-ger-in)
operation, die Operation (op'-er-ah-tee-own)
pain, der Schmerz (shmairts')
patient, der Patient (paht'-ee-ent)
poison, das Gift (gift)
policeman, der Schutzmann (shoots'-mun)
rash, der Ausschlag (owce-shlahg)
scar, die Narbe (nahr'-ber)
sick, to feel, sich schlecht fühlen (sich shlecht fül'-en)
sling, die Schlinge (shling'-er)
sore, schmerzhaft (shmairts-haft)
splint, die Schiene (sheen'-er)
spot, der Pickel (pick'-el)
sprain, die Verrenkung (fair-renk'-ōōng)
sting, der Stich (shtich)
stomach-ache, Magenschmerzen (mah'-gen-shmair-tsen)
sty(e), das Gerstenkorn (gair'-sten-korn)
sunstroke, der Sonnenstich (zonn'-en-shtich)
surgeon, der Chirurg (shee'-roorg)
swelling, die Geschwulst (ger'-shvōōlst)
temperature, die Temperatur (tem'-pay-rah-toor)
throat, der Hals (huls)

toothache, die Zahnschmerzen (tsahn'-shmairts-en)
treatment, die Behandlung (ber'-hunt-lŏŏng)
vomit, to, erbrechen (air-brech-en)
waiting-room, das Wartezimmer (vart'-er-tsimm'-er)
wound, die Wunde (vŏŏnd'er)
x-ray, to, röntgen (rurnt'-shen)

There has been an accident	Hier war ein Unfall
	here var ine ŏŏn'-fal
Send for a policeman (doctor, ambulance)	Rufen Sie einen Schutzmann (Arzt, Krankenwagen)
	roof'-en z ee i'-nen shoots'-mun (artst, krunk'-en-vahg'-en)
Is there a doctor here?	Ist ein Arzt hier?
	ist ine artst here
Someone has fallen in the water	Jemand ist ins Wasser gefallen
	yay'-munt ist ins vuss'-er ger'-full'-en
He is seriously injured	Er ist schwer verletzt
	air ist shvair fair-letst
He has been run over	Er ist überfahren worden
	air ist ü'-ber-fahr'-en vŏrd'-en
He is losing blood	Er blutet
	air bloot'-et
He has fainted	Er ist ohnmächtig geworden
	air ist own-mech'-tich ger'-vŏrd'-en
Are you all right?	Sind Sie unverletzt?
	zint zee ŏŏn'-fair-letst
Can anyone speak English?	Spricht jemand englisch?
	shpricht yay'-munt eng'-lish
I do not understand	Ich verstehe nicht
	ich fair-shtay'-er nicht
I feel better now	Es geht mir besser
	ez gate mere bess'-er
It's all right; I am only shaken (bruised)	Es macht nichts; ich habe mich nur erschrocken (zerstossen)
	ez maCHt nichts; ich hah'-ber mich nŏŏr air-shrock'-en (tsersh-tō'-sen)

I just want to sit down for a while | Ich will mich nur etwas hinsetzen
ich vill mich noor et'-vuss hin'-zets-en

Can you dress this wound? | Können Sie die Wunde verbinden?
Kurn'-en zee dee vōŏnd'-er fair-bind'-en

Can you make a splint? | Können Sie eine Schiene machen?
kurn'-en zee i'-ner sheen'-er maCH'-en

Help me to carry him (her) | Helfen Sie mir ihn (sie) zu tragen
hell'-fen zee mere een (zee) tsoo trahg'-en

Where is the nearest doctor (chemist)? | Wo ist der nächste Arzt (die nächste Apotheke)?
vō ist dair next'-er (artst, dee next'-er up-ō-tay'-ker)

Please take this; I am deeply grateful to you | Bitte nehmen Sie das; ich bin Ihnen sehr dankbar
bitt'-er nay'-men zee duss; ich bin ee'-nen zair dunk'-bar

My leg is very painful | Mein Bein tut sehr weh
mine bine toot zair vay

It hurts me here | Es tut mir hier weh
ez toot mere here vay

I can't move | Ich kann mich nicht bewegen
ich kun mich nicht bev-ay'-gen

I have broken my ankle | Ich habe den Knöchel gebrochen
ich hah'-ber dane k-nurch'-el geb-roCH'-en

I have cut my wrist | Ich habe mir das Handgelenk zerschnitten
ich hah'-ber mere duss hunt'-gel-enk tsair-shnitt'-en

He (she) has burnt his (her) hand | Er (sie) hat sich seine (ihre) Hand verbrannt
air (zee) hut zich sī'-ner (eer'-er) hunt fair-brunt

He has a nasty cut on the head — Er hat einen schlimmen Schnitt auf dem Kopf

air hut i'-nen shlimm'-en shnitt owf dame kopf

I have a pain in . . . — Ich habe Schmerzen in . . .

ich hah'-ber shmairts'-en in . .

I feel faint — Ich fühle mich schwach

ich fü'-ler mich shvaCH

I have a bad cold — Ich bin sehr erkältet

ich bin zair air-kelt'-et

I have a sore throat (headache, influenza) — Ich habe Halsschmerzen (Kopfschmerzen, die Grippe)

ich hah'-ber huls'-shmairts-en (kopf'-shmairts-en, dee grip'-er)

I have no appetite. I have indigestion — Ich habe keinen Appetit. Ich habe Verdauungsstörungen

ich hah'-ber ki'-nen a'-pe-tit. ich hah'-ber fair-dow-öong-shtur-öong'-en

He has a temperature — Er hat Fieber

air hut fee'-ber

My nose is bleeding — Meine Nase blutet

mi'-ner nah'-zer bloot'-et

I think I have food poisoning — Ich glaube ich habe Speisevergiftung

ich glow'-ber ich hah'-ber spi'-zer-fair-gift-öong

Where should I have this prescription made up? — Wo kann ich dieses Rezept hergestellt bekommen?

voh kun ich dee'-zes ray-tsept hair'-ger-shtellt ber'-komm'-en

Can I get up, or must I stay in in bed? — Kann ich aufstehen, oder muss ich im Bett bleiben?

kun ich owf'-shtay-en, ō'-der mööss ich im bett bli'-ben

How long must I stay in bed? — Wie lange muss ich im Bett bleiben?

vee lung'-er mööss ich im bett bli'-ben

Can you get me a nurse? — Können Sie mir eine Pflegerin beschaffen?

kurn'-en zee mere i'-ner pflay'-ger-in ber'-shuff'-en

Shall I be fit to travel on Wednesday ?	Werde ich Mittwoch reisen können?

vair'-der ich mitt'-voCH rī'-zen kurn'-en

When will you come again ?	Wann kommen Sie wieder?

vun komm'-en zee vee'-der

What do I owe you ?	Was bin ich Ihnen schuldig?

vuss bin ich ee'-nen shōōl-dich

Can you recommend me a good dentist ?	Können Sie mir einen guten Zahnarzt empfehlen?

kurn'-en zee mere i'-nen goot'-en tsahn'-artst emp-fay'-len

What is his address ?	Wo wohnt er?

voh vōnt air

I have terrible toothache	Ich habe schreckliche Zahn-schmerzen

ich hah'-ber shreck'-lich-er tsahn'-shmairts-en

I have had it for three days now	Ich habe sie schon seit drei Tagen

ich hah'-ber zee shone zite dry tahg'-en

I have lost a filling	Ich habe eine Plombe verloren

ich hah'-ber i'-ner plom'-ber fair-lö'-ren

The nerve hurts	Der Nerv tut weh

dair nairf toot vay

The gums are so sore	Das Zahnfleisch tut so weh

duss tsahn'-flīsh toot zo vay

You are hurting me	Sie tuen mir weh

zee too'-en mere vay

Can I have an injection?	Kann ich eine Spritze haben?

kun ich i'-ner shprit'-ser hah'-ben

I have broken my plate	Ich habe meine Gaumen-platte zerbrochen

ich hah'-ber mi'-ner gow'-men-plutt'-er tsair-brōCH'-en

My plate hurts	Meine Gaumenplatte drückt

mi'-ner gow'-men-platt'-er drückt

Must the tooth come out ?	Muss der Zahn gezogen werden?
	mōoss dair tsahn ger-tsō'-gen vaird'-en
I want this tooth filled	Ich möchte diesen Zahn plombiert haben
	ich murcht'-er dee'-zen tsahn plom-beert' hah'-ben
That hurts	Das tut weh
	duss toot vay
Am I to come again ?	Muss ich wiederkommen?
	mooss ich vee'-der-komm'-en
I am leaving here on the . . .	Ich reise am . . . ab
	ich ri'-zer um . . . up

VISITING FRIENDS

Is this where . . . lives ?	Wohnt . . . hier?
	vōnt . . . here
Is he (she) at home ?	Ist er (sie) zu Hause?
	ist air (zee) tsoo how'-zer
It is Mr. (Mrs., Miss) . . .	Mein Name ist . . . (without prefix)
	mine nah'-mer ist . . .
May I introduce myself, I am . . .	Darf ich mich vorstellen; Mein Name ist . . .
	darf ich mich fore'-shtell-en; mine nah'-mer ist . . .
Delighted to meet you	Sehr angenehm
	zair un'-gen-aim
How do you do ?	Wie geht es Ihnen?
	vee gate ez ee'-nen
Welcome to England (Germany)	Willkommen in England (Deutschland)
	vill-komm'-en in eng'-lunt (doytsh'-lunt)

I am Mr. Smith, and this is my wife

Ich bin Mr. Smith und das ist meine Frau

ich bin Mr. Smith ŏŏnt duss ist mi'-ner frow

Did you have a good journey?

Haben Sie eine gute Reise gehabt?

hah'-ben zee i'-ner goot'-er ri'-zer ger'-habt

This is your bedroom and here is the bathroom (lavatory)

Das ist Ihr Schlafzimmer und hier ist das Badezimmer (Toilette)

duss ist eer shlahf-tsimm'-er ŏŏnt here ist duss bahd'-er-tsimm'-er (twa'-lett'-er)

Do you need anything?

Brauchen Sie noch etwas?

browCH'-en zee noCH et'-vuss

Are you tired (hungry, thirsty)?

Sind Sie müde (haben Sie Hunger, Durst)?

zint zee mü'-der (hah'-ben zee hŏŏng'-er, doorst)

Is there anything you can't eat?

Können Sie irgendetwas nicht essen?

kurn'-en zee eer-gent-et'-vuss nicht ess'-en

Will you help me with the shopping (housework, washing-up)?

Würden Sie mir mit dem Einkaufen (im Haushalt, mit dem Abwaschen) helfen

würd'-en zee mere mit dame ine-kowf'-en (im house-hult, mit dame up'-vush'-en) hell'-fen

Will you look after the baby (children)?

Passen Sie bitte auf das Baby (die Kinder) auf?

puss'-en zee bitt'-er owf duss baby (dee kint'-er) owf

Can I go out for the day on Sunday?

Kann ich den ganzen Sonntag frei haben?

kun ich dane gunts'-en zonn'-tahg fry hah'-ben

When can I go out in the evening?

Wann kann ich abends ausgehen?

vunn kun ich ah-bents owce'-gay-en

Can I go to the cinema this evening? / Darf ich heute abend ins Kino gehen?

Darf ich hoy'-ter ah'-bent ins keen'-o gay'-en

Where can I enrol for English (German) classes? / Wo kann ich mich für englische (deutsche) Stunden anmelden?

voh kun ich mich für eng'-lish'-er (doytsh'-er) shtoond'-en un'-meld'-en

Where is the Catholic (Protestant) church? / Wo ist die katholische (evangelische) Kirche?

voh ist dee kah'-toh-lish'-er (e-fun-gay-lish'-er) kirch'-er

Have you written to your parents? / Haben Sie an Ihre Eltern geschrieben?

hah'-ben zee un ee'-rer el'-tern ger'-shree-ben

I have a letter for you from . . . / Ich habe einen Brief für Sie von . . .

ich hah'-ber i'-nen brief für zee fon . . .

I should like to very much / Sehr gern

zair gairn

Will you call for me at my hotel? / Wollen Sie mich von meinem Hotel abholen?

voll'-en zee mich fon mi'-nem ho-tell' up'-hole-en

When shall we meet? / Wann sollen wir uns treffen?

vunn zoll'-en vere ööns treff'-en

When shall I see you again? / Wann werde ich Sie wiedersehen?

vunn vair'-der ich zee vee'-der zay'-en

Thank you very much / Ich danke Ihnen vielmals

ich dunk'-er ee'-nen feel'-mulce

I am so glad to have met you / Ich freue mich, Sie kennengelernt zu haben

ich froy'-er mich, zee kenn'-en gel-airnt tsoo hah'-ben

The pleasure is mine / Ganz meinerseits

gunts mi'-ner-ziten

Please take my address and let me know if you are coming to ...

Bitte, notieren Sie meine Adresse, und schreiben Sie mir, wenn Sie nach . . . kommen

bitt'-er no-teer'-en zee mī'-ner a-dress'-er ōōnt shrī'-ben zee mere, venn zee naCH ... kōmm'-en

MONEY

In Germany the basic unit of currency is the *Deutsche Mark* (doytsh'er mark) called D Mark (day'-mark) which is divided into 100 *Pfennig*.

In Austria the unit of currency is the *Schilling* (shilling). One *Schilling* contains 100 *Groschen* (grosh'-en).

In Switzerland the unit of currency is the *Swiss franc*. The *centime* (one-hundredth part of the franc) is called in German-speaking Switzerland *Rappen*, though the word *centime* is understood.

VOCABULARY

bank, die Bank (bunk)
bank manager, der Bankvorsteher (bunk-fore-stay'-er)
change (small), das Kleingeld (kline-gelt)
change, to, wechseln (vex'-eln)
cash, to, einwechseln (īne-vex'-eln)
cheque (traveller's) der Reisescheck (rī'-zer-sheck)
coin, die Münze (mün'-tse)
draw, to, abheben (up'-hay-ben)
letter of credit, der Kreditbrief (kray-deet'-brief)
money, das Geld (gelt)
note, die Banknote (bunk-note'-er)
rate of exchange, der Wechselkurs (vex'-el-koors)
signature, die Unterschrift (ōōn'-ter-shrift)

Is there a bank near here?

Ist eine Bank in der Nähe?

ist ī'-ner bunk in dair nay'-her

Which is the way to the ... bank?

Wie komme ich zur ... Bank?

vee komm'-er ich tsoor ... bank

Where can I cash a traveller's cheque?

Wo kann ich einen Reisescheck einlösen?

voh kun ich ī-nen rī'-zer-sheck īne-lurs'-en

I want to cash a traveller's cheque	Ich möchte einen Reisescheck einlösen

ich murch'-ter i'-nen ri'-zer-sheck ine-lurs'-en

What is the rate of exchange today?	Wie steht der Wechselkurs heute?

vee stayt dair vex'-el-koors hoyt'-er

I have a letter of credit	Ich habe einen Kreditbrief

ich hah'-ber i'-nen kray-deet'-brief

I want to draw . . .	Ich möchte . . . abheben

ich murch'-ter . . . up'-hay-ben

Can I see the manager?	Kann ich den Vorsteher sprechen?

kun ich dane fore'-shtay-er shprech'-en

Can you change 50 marks for me?	Können Sie mir fünfzig Mark wechseln?

kurn'-en zee mere fünf'-tsich mark vex'-eln

Give me two notes and some small change	Geben Sie mir zwei Noten und etwas Kleingeld

gay'-ben zee mere tsvī note'-n ŏont et'-vuss kline-gelt

I think you have made a mistake	Ich glaube Sie haben sich verrechnet

ich glow'-ber zee hah'-ben zich fair'-rech'-net

TABLES

The traveller should insert the rates of exchange.

GERMANY

5 Pfennig=	20 Mark=
10 Pfennig=	50 Mark=
50 Pfennig=	100 Mark=
1 Mark =	500 Mark=
5 Mark =	1,000 Mark=

AUSTRIA

5 Groschen=	20 Schillinge=
10 Groschen=	50 Schillinge=
50 Groschen=	100 Schillinge=
1 Schilling =	500 Schillinge=
5 Schillinge=	1,000 Schillinge=

SWITZERLAND

1 centime =	20 francs=
10 centimes=	50 francs=
50 centimes=	100 francs=
1 franc =	500 francs=
5 francs =	1,000 francs=

NUMBERS

1 = eins (ince)
2 = zwei (tsvī)
3 = drei (dry)
4 = vier (fear)
5 = fünf (fünf)
6 = sechs (zex)
7 = sieben (zee'-ben)
8 = acht (aCHt)
9 = neun (noyn)
10 = zehn (tsain)
11 = elf (elf)
12 = zwölf (tsvurlf)
13 = dreizehn (dry'-tsain)
14 = vierzehn (fear'-tsain)
15 = fünfzehn (fünf'-tsain)
16 = sechzehn (zech'-tsain)
17 = siebzehn (zeep'-tsain)
18 = achtzehn (aCHt'-tsain)
19 = neunzehn (noyn'-tsain)
20 = zwanzig (tsvun'-tsich)

```
        21 = einundzwanzig (īne'-oont-tsvun'-tsich)
        30 = dreissig (dry'-sich)
        40 = vierzig (fear'-tsich)
        50 = fünfzig (fünf'-tsich)
        60 = sechzig (zech'-tsich)
        70 = siebzig (zeep'-tsich)
        80 = achtzig (aCHt'-tsich)
        90 = neunzig (noyn'-tsich)
       100 = hundert (hoŏn'-dert)
       200 = zweihundert (tsvī-hoŏn'-dert)
     1,000 = tausend (tow'-zent)
     2,000 = zweitausend (tsvī-tow-zent)
 1,000,000 = eine Million (ī'-ner mill-i-ōn')
```

```
       1st = erste (airst'-er)
       2nd = zweite (tsvī'-ter)
       3rd = dritte (dritt'-er)
       4th = vierte (fear'-ter)
       5th = fünfte (fünf'-ter)
      10th = zehnte (tsain'-ter)
      11th = elfte (elf-ter)
      20th = zwanzigste (tsvun'-tsich-ster)
      21st = einundzwanzigste (ine-oŏnt-tsvun'-tsich-ster)
      50th = fünfzigste (fünf'-tsich-ster)
     100th = hundertste (hoŏn'-dert-ster)
```

a half = Halb (hulp)
a third = ein Drittel (ine dritt'-el)
a quarter = ein Viertel (ine fear'-tel)
a fifth = ein Fünftel (ine fünf'-tel)
three-quarters, dreiviertel (dry-feer-tel)
two-thirds, zwei Drittel (tsvī dritt'-el)
an eighth, ein Achtel (aCHt'-el)

1950 = neunzehnhundertfünfzig (noyn'-tsain-hoŏn-dert-fünf-tsich)
1962 = neunzehnhundertzweiundsechzig (noyn'-tsain-hoŏn-dert-tsvī-oŏnt-zech'-tsich)
page 63 = Seite dreiundsechzig (zī'-ter dry'-oŏnt-zech'-tsich)
number 426 = Nummer vierhundertsechsundzwanzig (noŏm'-er fear'-hoŏn-dert-zex-oŏnt-tsvun'-tsich)

CONVERSION TABLES

DISTANCE

Kilometres		Miles	Miles		Kilometres
1	approx.	$\frac{5}{8}$	1	approx.	1·6
2	,,	$1\frac{1}{4}$	2	,,	3·2
3	,,	$1\frac{7}{8}$	3	,,	4·8
4	,,	$2\frac{1}{2}$	4	,,	6·4
5	,,	$3\frac{1}{8}$	5	,,	8
6	,,	$3\frac{3}{4}$	6	,,	9·6
7	,,	$4\frac{3}{8}$	7	,,	11·3
8	,,	5	8	,,	12·9
9	,,	$5\frac{5}{8}$	9	,,	14·5
10	,,	$6\frac{1}{4}$	10	,,	16·1
15	,,	$9\frac{3}{8}$	15	,,	24·1
20	,,	$12\frac{1}{2}$	20	,,	32·2
25	,,	$15\frac{5}{8}$	25	,,	40·2
30	,,	$18\frac{3}{4}$	30	,,	48·3
35	,,	$21\frac{7}{8}$	35	,,	56·3
40	,,	25	40	,,	64·4
45	,,	$28\frac{1}{8}$	45	,,	72·4
50	,,	$31\frac{3}{8}$	50	,,	80·5
55	,,	$34\frac{3}{8}$	55	,,	88·5
60	,,	$37\frac{1}{2}$	60	,,	96·6
65	,,	$40\frac{5}{8}$	65	,,	104·6
70	,,	$43\frac{3}{4}$	70	,,	112·7
75	,,	$46\frac{7}{8}$	75	,,	120·7
80	,,	50	80	,,	128·7
85	,,	$53\frac{1}{8}$	85	,,	136·8
90	,,	$56\frac{1}{4}$	90	,,	144·8
95	,,	$59\frac{3}{8}$	95	,,	152·9
100	,,	$62\frac{1}{2}$	100	,,	161

N.B. A rough way to convert kilometres to miles : divide the kilometres by 8 and multiply by 5. E.g. 32 kms. ÷ 8 = 4 × 5 = 20 miles.

Vice versa, to convert miles to kilometres divide by 5 and multiply by 8. e.g. 35 miles ÷ 5 = 7 × 8 = 56 kms.

WEIGHTS AND MEASURES

VOCABULARY

depth, die Tiefe (teef'-er)
height, die Höhe (hurh'-er)
length, die Länge (leng'-er)
measure, to, messen (mess'-en)
thickness, die Stärke (shtairk'-er)
weight, das Gewicht (ger'-vicht)
width (breadth), die Weite (vite-er)

What is the depth of . . .?   Wie tief ist . . .?

vee teef ist . . .

It is five metres long by ten   Es ist fünf Meter lang und
metres wide   zehn Meter breit

ez ist fünf may'-ter lung öönt tsain may'-ter brite

WEIGHTS

Gramme		Ounces	Ounces		Gramme
50	approx.	1¾	1	approx.	28
100	,,	3½	2	,,	56
125	,,	4¼	5	,,	142
250	,,	8¾	8 (½ lb.)	,,	227
500 (1 Pfund)	,,	1 lb. 1½	12	,,	340
1,000 (1 Kilo)	,,	2 lb. 3	16 (1 lb.)	,,	453

Kilo		Pounds	Stones		Kilo
5	approx.	10¾	1 (14 lb.)	approx.	6·35
10	,,	21½	7 (98 lb.)	,,	44·5
15	,,	32¼	8 (112 lb.)	,,	51
20	,,	43	9 (126 lb.)	,,	57
25	,,	54¼	10 (140 lb.)	,,	63·5
30	,,	64½	11 (154 lb.)	,,	70
40	,,	86	12 (168 lb.)	,,	76
50	,,	108½	13 (182 lb.)	,,	82·5
75	,,	162¾	14 (196 lb.)	,,	89
100	,,	220	15 (210 lb.)	,,	95

LIQUID MEASURES

1 Litre $= 1\frac{3}{4}$ pint
$4\frac{1}{2}$ Litre $= 1$ gallon

LENGTH

1 Centimetre $= \frac{2}{5}$ inch
$2\frac{1}{2}$ Centimetre $= 1$ inch
30 Centimetre $= 1$ foot
91 Centimetre $= 1$ yard
1 Metre $= 39$ inches

PRESSURE (TYRES)

Lb. per sq. in.		Kg. per sq. cm.	Kg. per sq. cm.		Lb. per sq. in.
16	approx.	1·12	1·1	approx.	16·0
18	,,	1·27	1·3	,,	18·5
20	,,	1·41	1·4	,,	19·9
22	,,	1·55	1·6	,,	22·8
24	,,	1·69	1·7	,,	24·2
26	,,	1·83	1·8	,,	25·6
28	,,	1·97	2·0	,,	28·4
30	,,	2·11	2·1	,,	29·9

ALTITUDE

Metres		Feet	Feet		Metres
25	approx.	82	50	approx.	15
50	,,	164	75	,,	23
75	,,	246	100	,,	31
100	,,	328	250	,,	76
250	,,	820	500	,,	152
500	,,	1,640	1,000	,,	305
1,000	,,	3,281	2,000	,,	610
2,000	,,	6,562	3,000	,,	915
3,000	,,	9,843	4,000	,,	1,220
4,000	,,	13,124	5,000	,,	1,525

N.B. To convert metres roughly to yards multiply by 12 and divide by 11.
e.g. 100 metres $\times 12 = 1,200 \div 11 = 109$ yards.

TEMPERATURE

Fahrenheit °F	Centigrade °C	Fahrenheit °F	Centigrade °C
212 (Boiling)	100	59	15
104	40	50	10
102	38·9	41	5
101	38·3	32 (Freezing)	0
100	37·8	28	− 2
98·4 (Body)	37	23	− 5
97	36·1	18	− 8
86	30	12	− 11
80	26·7	5	− 15
77	25	0	− 18
68	20	− 4	− 20
64	17·8		

CLOTHING SIZES

DRESSES AND SUITS (Women)

British	36	38	40	42	44	46
American	34	36	38	40	42	44
Continental	42	44	46	48	50	52

DRESSES AND SUITS (Junior Miss)

British	32	33	35	36	38	39
American	10	12	14	16	18	20
Continental	38	40	42	44	46	48

MEN'S SUITS AND OVERCOATS

British and American	36	38	40	42	44	46
Continental	46	48	50	52	54	56

SHIRTS

British and American	14	$14\frac{1}{2}$	15	$15\frac{1}{2}$	16	$16\frac{1}{2}$	17
Continental	36	37	38	39	41	42	43

SOCKS

British and American	9½	10	10½	11	11½
Continental	38-39	39-40	40-41	41-42	42-43

HATS

British and American	6½	6⅝	6¾	6⅞	7	7⅛	7¼	7⅜	7½
Continental	53	54	55	56	57	58	59	60	61

SHOES

British and American	3	4	5	6	7	8	9	10
Continental	36	37	38	39	41	42	43	44

STOCKINGS

British and American	8	8½	9	9½	10	10½
Continental	0	1	2	3	4	5

GLOVE sizes are the same in every country.

COUNTRIES AND NATIONALITIES

Country	Inhabitant
Africa, Afrika (ahf′-ree-kah)	**African,** Afrikaner (ahf′-ree-kahn′-er)
America, Amerika (um-air′-ee-ka)	**American,** Amerikaner (um-air′-ee-kah′-ner)
Austria, Österreich (u*r*st′-er-rīch)	**Austrian,** Österreicher (u*r*st′-er-rīch-er)
Australia, Australien (ows-trahl′-ee-en)	**Australian,** Australier (ows-trahl′-ee-er)
Belgium, Belgien (belg′-ee-en)	**Belgian,** Belgier (belg′-ee-er)
Canada, Kanada (kun′-ah-dah)	**Canadian,** Kanadier (kun′-ahd′-ee-er)
China, China (shee-nah)	**Chinaman,** Chinese (shee-nay′-ze*r*)
Czechoslovakia, Tschechoslawakei (chech-o-slo-vah-kī′)	**Czech,** Tscheche (chech′-e*r*)
Denmark, Dänemark (dane′-er-mark)	**Dane,** Däne (dane-e*r*)
England, England (eng′-lunt)	**Englishman,** Engländer (eng′-lend-er)
Finland, Finnland (fin′-lunt)	**Finn,** Finnländer (fin′-lend-er)

France, Frankreich (frunk'-rīch)

Germany, Deutschland (doytsh'-lunt)

Greece, Griechenland (greech'-en-lunt)

Holland, Holland (holl'-unt)
Hungary, Ungarn (ōōng'-garn)
Ireland, Ireland (eer'-lunt)
Italy, Italien (it-ahl'-ee-en)
Norway, Norwegen (nor'-vay-gen)

Poland, Polen (pole'-en)
Portugal, Portugal (por'-too-gal)

Russia, Russland (Rōōss'-lunt)
Scotland, Schottland (shot'-lunt)
Spain, Spanien (shpah'-nee-en)
Sweden, Schweden (shvay'-den)
Switzerland, Schweiz (in Switzerland—in der Schweiz) (shvīts)
Turkey, Türkei (tür'-ky)
Wales, Wales (wales)
Yugoslavia, Jugoslawien (yu-gos-lah'-vien)

Frenchman, Franzose (frun-tso'-zer)
German, Deutscher (doytsh'-er)

Greek, Grieche (greech'-er)

Dutchman, Holländer (holl-end'-er)
Hungarian, Ungar (ōōng'-gar)
Irishman, Ire (eer'-er)
Italian, Italiener (it-ahl-ee-ain'-er)
Norwegian, Norweger (nor-vay'-ger)

Pole, Pole (pole'-er)
Portuguese, Portugiese (por'-too-gee'-zer)
Russian, Russe (rōōss'-er)
Scotsman, Schotte (shot'-ter)
Spaniard, Spanier (shpah'-nee-er)
Swede, Schwede (shvay'-der)
Swiss, Schweizer (shvīts'-er)

Turk, Türke (türk'-er)
Welshman, Waliser (val-eez'-er)
Yugoslavian, Jugoslawe (yu-gos-lah'-ver)

GEOGRAPHICAL NAM...

north, Norden (nord'-en)
south, Süden (züd'-en)
east, Osten (ost'-en)
west, Westen (vest'-en)

Bavaria, Bayern (by-ern)
Black Forest, der Schwarzwald (shvarts-valt)
Brunswick, Braunschweig (brown-shvīg)
Brussels, Brüssel (brü'-sel)
Carinthia, Kärnten (kairn'-ten)
Cologne, Köln (kurln)
Danube, die Donau (doh-now)
Flushing, Vlissingen (fliss'-ing-en)
Geneva, Genf (genf)
Lake Constance, der Bodensee (boh'-den-zay)
Lake Lucerne, der Vierwaldstättersee (fear-valt-shtett-er-zay)
Munich, München (mün'-chen)
Vienna, Wien (veen)

REGISTER

INDEX